D1362749

# WebPlus X6
# Resource Guide

# Contacting Serif

Our support mission is to provide fast, friendly technical advice and support from a team of experts.

### Serif Support on the web
Serif Support website:        support.serif.com

Twitter:        twitter.com/serifsupport

Facebook:        facebook.com/SerifSupport

### Additional Serif information
Serif website:        www.serif.com

Forums:        forums.serif.com

YouTube:        youtube.com/serifsoftware

### Main office (UK, Europe):
The Software Centre, PO Box 2000, Nottingham, NG11 7GW, UK

Main:        (0115) 914 2000

Registration (UK only):        (0800) 376 1989

Sales (UK only):        (0800) 376 7070

General Fax:        (0115) 914 2020

### North American office (US, Canada):
Registration:        (800) 794-6876

Sales:        (800) 489-6703

Customer Service:        (800) 489-6720

Support:        (603) 886-6642

### International enquiries
Please contact our main office.

# Credits

This Resource Guide, and the software described in it, is furnished under an end user License Agreement, which is included with the product. The agreement specifies the permitted and prohibited uses.

## Trademarks

Serif is a registered trademark of Serif (Europe) Ltd.

WebPlus is a registered trademark of Serif (Europe) Ltd.

All Serif product names are trademarks of Serif (Europe) Ltd.

Microsoft, Windows, and the Windows logo are registered trademarks of Microsoft Corporation. All other trademarks acknowledged.

Windows Vista and the Windows Vista Start button are trademarks or registered trademarks of Microsoft Corporation in the United States and/or other countries.

Google+ social service, Google Analytics web analytics service, and Google AdSense advertising service are trademarks of Google Inc.

## Copyrights

Digital Images ©2008 Hemera Technologies Inc. All Rights Reserved.

Digital Images ©2008 Jupiterimages Corporation, All Rights Reserved.

Digital Images ©2008 Jupiterimages France SAS, All Rights Reserved.

Content ©2008 Jupiterimages Corporation. All Rights Reserved.

Portions images ©1997-2002 Nova Development Corporation; ©1995 Expressions Computer Software; ©1996-98 CreatiCom, Inc.; ©1996 Cliptoart; ©1997 Multimedia Agency Corporation; ©1997-98 Seattle Support Group. Rights of all parties reserved.

This application was developed using LEADTOOLS, copyright © 1991-2007 LEAD Technologies, Inc. ALL Rights Reserved.

THE PROXIMITY HYPHENATION SYSTEM © 1989 Proximity Technology Inc. All rights reserved.

THE PROXIMITY/COLLINS DATABASEÒ © 1990 William Collins Sons & Co. Ltd.; © 1990 Proximity Technology Inc. All rights reserved.

THE PROXIMITY/MERRIAM-WEBSTER DATABASEÒ © 1990 Merriam-Webster Inc.; © 1990 Proximity Technology Inc. All rights reserved.

The Sentry Spelling-Checker Engine © 2000 Wintertree Software Inc.

The ThesDB Thesaurus Engine © 1993-97 Wintertree Software Inc.

# Introduction

Welcome to the WebPlus X6 Resource Guide! Whether you are new to WebPlus or a seasoned website designer, the Resource Guide is something you'll return to time and time again.

The Resource Guide offers a range of exciting tutorials and full-colour previews of professionally designed content (including instructions on how to access it) to help you get the best out of WebPlus X6.

The Resource Guide is organized into the following chapters:

## 1: Tutorials

Illustrated, step-by-step training to help you get started with WebPlus, along with more complex projects to enhance your website design skills.

## 2: Navigation Bars

Previews of customizable, dynamic navigation bars which can be quickly added to your website.

## 3: Colour Schemes

Previews of customizable colour schemes that can transform your site's appearance in an instant.

## 4: Theme Layouts

Previews of theme layouts to use as a starting point for your website—just add your own pictures and text.

## 5: Pro Templates

Previews of design templates complete with royalty-free pictures to get your website launched as quickly as possible—just add your own text.

# Contents

## Chapter 1 - Tutorials      1

## Chapter 2 - Navigation Bars      225

## Chapter 3 - Colour Schemes      241

## Chapter 4 - Theme Layouts      255

## Chapter 5 - Pro Templates      319

# Tutorials

Whether you are new to **Serif WebPlus X6** or an experienced user, these tutorials will help you to get the best out of the program.

As a new user, we recommend that you follow the tutorials in order as they will introduce you to the different concepts gradually. If you have used other Serif products, you'll find that many of the tools will already have a familiar feel.

Whatever your level of experience, you will be able to complete the tutorials if you follow the steps.

Have fun!

# Accessing the tutorials

You can access the tutorials in one of the following ways:

- From the WebPlus X6 Startup Wizard, select from the **Learn** section. Different icons indicate the type of tutorial available.

a video tutorial

an online tutorial

see more tutorials and videos!

- or -

- From WebPlus, click **Help** and then click **Tutorials**.

## Accessing the sample files

Throughout the tutorials, you'll be prompted to access sample files. All samples are accessible via the Internet at the following location:

http://go.serif.com/resources/WPX6

If you've clicked on a file, you can either open or save the file. We recommend you save the file to your desktop or a named folder on your computer.

## Useful icons

Before we get started, here is a quick guide to the icons that you'll find useful along the way.

These give you an estimate of how long the tutorial will take to complete. Some tutorials are longer than others so this should help you put enough time aside to complete a tutorial.

Not sure how hard the tutorial is? Let the pencils guide you. Tutorials are graded between 1 (beginner) - 5 (advanced). This provides a guide to how much WebPlus experience you need to complete the tutorial. Don't worry though, nothing is impossible and you should always be able to follow the steps!

Don't forget to save your work! It's good practice to save often. We'll remind you along the way with these helpful save points.

When you see this icon, there are project files and/or images available for download that will help you to complete the tutorial. Sometimes we provide you with partially completed projects so that you can concentrate on the main learning point of the tutorial, without having to recreate our design.

This is a note. Notes provide useful information about the program or a particular technique.

This is a tip. Our tips provide information that will help you with your projects.

This is a warning! We don't want to make you panic but when you see this icon, you need to pay attention to the steps as they will be particularly important.

# Exploring WebPlus X6

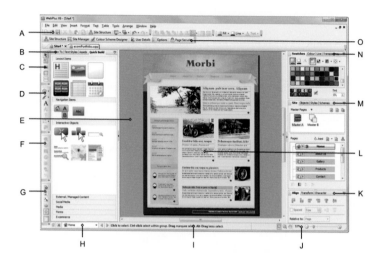

(A) Standard, Arrange and Colours toolbars, (B) How To, Text Styles, Assets and Quick Build tabs, (C) Basic toolbar, (D) Drawing toolbar, (E) Pasteboard area, (F) Web Properties toolbar, (G) Studio toolbar, (H) Page Locator, (I) Hintline toolbar, (J) View toolbar, (K) Align, Transform and Character tabs, (L) Page area, (M) Site, Objects, Styles and Schemes tabs, (N) Swatches, Colour, Line and Transparency tabs, (M) Context toolbar.

## The WebPlus workspace

The WebPlus workspace consists of:

- A page area (L), where you put the text, graphics, and other elements that you want to appear on the final Web page.

- A surrounding pasteboard area (E), where you can keep elements that are being prepared or waiting to be positioned on the page area. (This is not displayed when the site is published.)

- Horizontal and vertical **toolbars** and **tabs**, used to access WebPlus commands and tools.

Move the mouse pointer around the screen and you'll see popup **tooltips** that identify toolbar buttons and flyouts.

Right-click any object or page region to bring up a **context menu** of functions.

# New Site from Template

 15-20 min

Creating a website in WebPlus can be as simple as choosing and customizing a design template, a theme layout (as in this example), or you can start from scratch. The building blocks that go on to make up your website are saved as a project file which will eventually be published to the internet for all to see.

By the end of this tutorial you will be able to:

* Preview your template site.

* Add template pages using the Site and Assets tabs.

* Add a new blank page.

* Add page content using the Assets tab.

## Let's begin...

1.  On the **File** menu, click **Startup Wizard...**

2.  In the Create section, click **Use Design Template**.

3.  In the dialog:

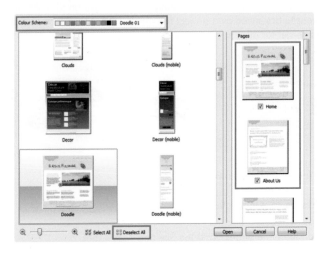

- In the **Theme Layouts** category, select **Doodle**.

- In the **Colour Scheme** drop-down list, select a scheme for your site—we've kept to the default scheme.

- At the bottom of the dialog, click ⊞ **Deselect All**.

- In the **Pages** pane, click to select the 'Home' and 'About Us' pages.

- Click **Open**.

The 'Home' page is displayed in the workspace with the **Assets** tab populated with all the theme's assets.

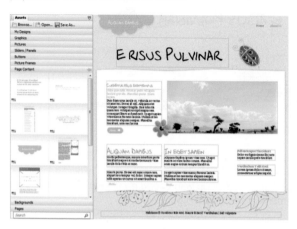

## To save your work:

1.  Before proceeding, click **File**, then **Save As...**

2.  Save your project file with a file name of your choice.

 Saving the WebPlus (.wpp) project file is not the same as publishing it as a website.

## To preview your site:

*   On the Standard toolbar, click the arrow to expand the 🖥️ ⁃ **Preview site** drop-down list.

    Select **Preview Site in {your web browser of choice}**. WebPlus generates the necessary temporary files and opens a new browser window displaying the site's Home page.

The navigation bar (highlighted) interconnects the site's pages and is an indispensable element of site design. Users will expect it to be there, they'll know what to do with it, and it will help them grasp your site's main content sections at a glance.

Once you've experimented with the navigation bar, close the browser window and return to WebPlus.

## Adding template pages

Your website will grow and change with your needs and you can add pages as you go. Blank pages can be added, but they need populating with content, which can be time consuming. More conveniently, you can add new template pages to your site. They come populated with professionally designed page content, saving you lots of time!

### To add a new template page:

1.   On the **Site** tab, click the arrow on the 📄 ▾ **Add new page or link** drop-down list and select **New Template Page...**

     The **Add New Page From Template** dialog will open with the **Doodle** theme layout displayed (if not, select it in the left-hand column).

**2.** In the dialog, in the **Pages** pane, click to select the 'Gallery' page.

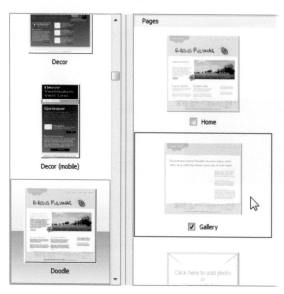

**3.** Click **Open** to add the page to your site.

The new 'Gallery' template page appears in the **Site** tab.

4.  On the **Site** tab, double-click on the 'Gallery' page to open it in the workspace.

Now, let's explore another way of adding pre-designed pages to your site—this time using the **Assets** tab.

 Don't forget to save your work!

### To add a new asset page:

1.  On the **Assets** tab, click the **Pages** category header to display the template's Page assets.

**2.** Drag the 'Contact Us' page onto the workspace, and drop it (by releasing the mouse button) to the right of the 'Gallery' page when a large arrow appears.

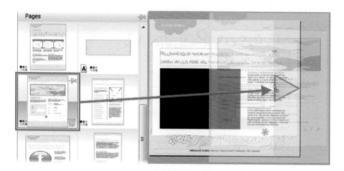

The page is added after the 'Gallery' page in the **Site** tab, listed as 'Page 4'.

**3.** On the **Site** tab, right-click 'Page 4' and select **Page Properties...**

**4.** In the **Page Properties** dialog, in the **Navigation** category, type 'Contact Us' into the **Page name** box, then click **OK**.

5. Preview your site in a browser to see your changes.

The navigation bar has automatically updated to accommodate your new Gallery and Contact Us pages.

Once you've experimented with the navigation bar, close the browser window and return to WebPlus.

 Don't forget to save your work!

## Adding a new blank page

You can quickly construct site pages by adding page content assets available from the **Assets** tab. First, you'll need to add a new page to your website.

### To add a new blank page:

1. On the **Site** tab, click the arrow on the ⊞ ⁻ **Add new page or link** drop-down list and select **New Blank Page...**

2. In the **Page Properties** dialog, in the **Navigation** category:

   • In the **Naming** section, type in a page name, title, and file name—we chose to create a 'Services' page.

   • In the **Placement** section, select **After** and then, from the drop-down list, select **About Us**.

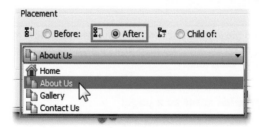

- Click **OK**.

Your new blank page opens in the workspace and is positioned after the 'About Us' page in the navigation bar and **Site** tab.

The new page automatically adopts all the page elements placed on the **Master A** page. This is indicated in the **Site** tab.

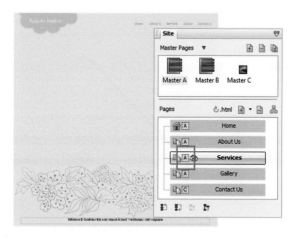

See *Understanding pages and master pages* in the WebPlus Help for more details on using Master pages.

## Adding page content

Now, we'll add the jagged white shape to this new page so it resembles the other pages on the site. This asset can be found in the Graphics category of the **Assets** tab.

### To add a graphic asset to a page:

1. On the **Assets** tab, click the **Graphics** category header to display the template's graphic assets.

2. Drag the bottom, right asset (the jagged white shape) onto the page.

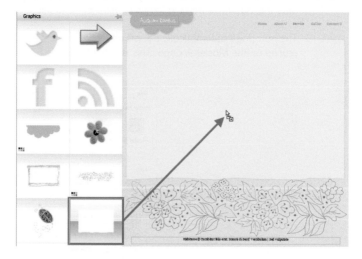

**3.** With the object still selected, drag on the top- and bottom-centre control handles to resize the shape to fill most of the page.

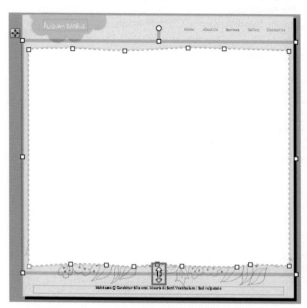

**4.** On the **Align** tab, click  **Centre Horizontally** to display the shape neatly on the page.

Now let's populate the page with page content!

### To add page content assets to a page:

1. On the **Assets** tab, click the **Page Content** category header to display the template's Page Content assets.

2. Drag any page content asset directly onto the page.

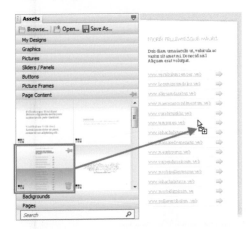

The page content is added to the page and remains selected.

Chances are you won't position the asset perfectly first time, so you may wish to reposition (and possibly resize) it once it is on the page.

### To reposition and resize assets:

1. With the Page Content asset still selected, click and drag the ⊕ button to reposition the content on the page.

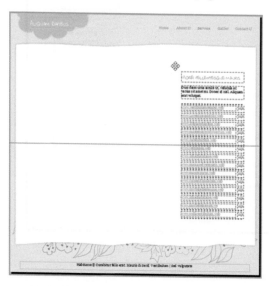

As you drag the content, dynamic guides will appear to allow you to line up content with the page (blue lines) or other content (red lines).

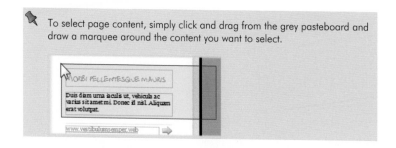

To select page content, simply click and drag from the grey pasteboard and draw a marquee around the content you want to select.

**2.**   Click the corner or side handles and drag them to resize page content as required.

 Elements within page content assets will resize differently, depending on their default behaviour. For example, frame text, artistic text, and graphics will all resize in different ways.

**3.** Drag additional page content items from the **Assets** tab onto the page, and reposition and resize as necessary—we added three page content assets in total and arranged them as illustrated below.

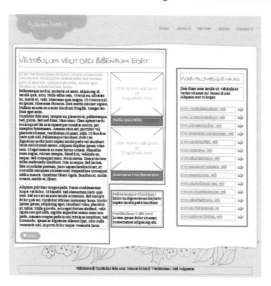

Your website is now ready to be populated with pictures, text, and hyperlinks!

Don't forget to save your work!

 Pictures, text, and hyperlinks are so important when building a website, we have dedicated tutorials for each of them, and therefore they are not discussed here. See the tutorials, *Pictures*, *Frame Text*, and *Creating Hyperlinks & Anchors*, on p. 65, p. 53, and p. 79, respectively, for more details.

With your website populated with custom pictures, text, and hyperlinks, all you need to do now is publish it to the internet! See the tutorial, *Previewing & Publishing*, on p. 195 for more details.

# Understanding Site Structure

 15-20 min

Using WebPlus, it's easy to design clearly structured websites that are quick and simple to navigate. In this tutorial, we'll use a WebPlus template to introduce you to the basic elements of site structure.

By the end of this tutorial you will be able to:

- Navigate between pages.

- Change navigation preferences.

- Rearrange pages.

- Create child pages.

## Let's begin...

1.   On the **File** menu, click **Startup Wizard...**

2.   In the Create section, click **Use Design Template**.

3.   In the **Theme Layouts** category, select **Vintage**.

4.   By default, all of the template pages are selected. This is fine for our
     example so click **Open**.

## Understanding site structure

When you build your website, it's important for you to have an
understanding of site structure and its hierarchy. This is a fundamental
part of website design and helps you to create a site that visitors will be
able to navigate easily.

To begin with, we'll have a look at the **Site** tab.

**To navigate between pages:**

1.  At the right of the workspace, click the **Site** tab. This tab displays the
    **Site Structure tree** for this particular site. You'll recognize the entries
    as the main pages of the site.

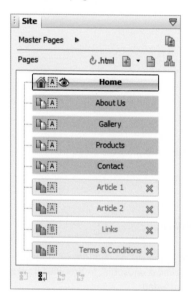

2.  Double-click a page entry to open it in the workspace.

    As you change pages, notice that the 👁 icon moves to indicate
    which page is currently in view and ready for editing.

**3.**   This time, in the **Site** tab, single-click any page entry to select it. Watch the **Site** tab and you'll see the ☀ icon indicating the page on view doesn't change. However, you can edit page properties and update other details of the highlighted page.

Let's take a few moments to examine the site we created from the template.

## Changing site navigation

If all of your pages were included in the site navigation, on a large website the navigation would be almost unusable. In WebPlus it's easy to specify whether or not a page is included.

In WebPlus, on the **Site** tab, pages that are not included in the navigation (highlighted) are lighter in colour, and have an 'x' next to their names.

If you preview the site in a browser, you can see this from the navigation bar.

## To preview your site in a browser:

1. On the Standard toolbar, click the arrow to expand the  **Preview site** drop-down list.

2. Select **Preview Site in** {your web browser of choice}.

3. Close the browser when you've finished.

Although the navigation bar updates on the page, it's useful to know how to preview it in a web browser. Once your site becomes more complicated and has different levels of navigation, previewing the site in a browser will become the easiest way to check the child-level navigation items.

## To change navigation options:

1. On the **Site** tab, right-click the 'Contact' page entry and click **Page Properties...**

2. In the **Page Properties** dialog, in the **Navigation** category, clear the **Include in Navigation** check box and then click **OK**.

In the **Site** tab the 'Contact' page entry has changed colour and now displays an 'x'.

Notice what happens in the navigation bar:

Switching off the **Include in Navigation** setting for a page forces navigation bars to ignore that page, and its button disappears.

3.  Open the **Page Properties** dialog again and select the **Include in Navigation** check box to reset it.

    On the page, you can see that the navigation bar has updated to include the 'Contact' page.

## Page order

The buttons at the bottom of the **Site** tab also allow you to quickly and easily change pages from child to parent, or to move pages up or down in the list. To use any of these buttons, select the page that you want to move and then click the relevant button.

### To change page order:

1.  On the **Site** tab, click to select the 'Gallery' page.

2.  Click the  **Move Page Up** button.

The page moves up the list while staying at the same hierarchy. If the page has child pages, these are also moved as they are dependent on the parent page. As this page is included in the navigation, the navigation bar updates automatically to mirror the new top-level page order.

## Child pages

A parent-and-child 'tree' structure provides a natural framework for organizing site content into sections and levels. This site currently has one main page at the top level for each of our main sections. Over time we would expect to add subsidiary (child) pages to each section. Let's do this now.

### To add a new child page:

1. On the **Site** tab, select the 'Products' page and click the arrow on the ⊞ ˅ **Add new page or link** drop-down list.

2. Click **New Blank Page...**

3. In the **Page Properties** dialog:

   - On the **Navigation** option, in the **Page name** text box, type 'Product 1'.

   - Change the **File name** to 'product1.html'.

   - In the **Placement** section, select the **Child of** option.

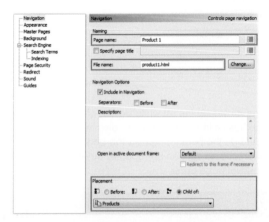

- Click **OK**.

A new page opens in the workspace and a new entry is displayed in the **Site** tab. The new page is indented under the 'Products' page, i.e., it's a child of the 'Products' page as we specified in the dialog.

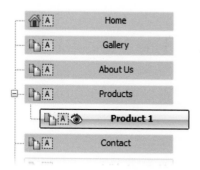

4. On the page, you'll see that the Products item on the navigation bar now has a small arrow next to it.

Preview the site in a browser. If you hover the over the Products item in the navigation bar, you'll now see a Product 1 item appear in the drop-down list.

 If you add a new template page to your site, you will need to manually change this to be a child page.

**To make an existing page a child page:**

1. On the **Site** tab, select the 'Gallery' page.

2. Click  Make Page a Child.

The page is made a child of the page above, in this example, a child of the 'Home' page.

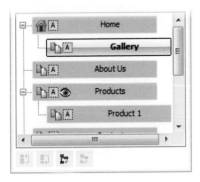

# Assets

 25 min

The **Assets** tab in WebPlus X6 plays host to a wide variety of designs and objects to help you to easily and quickly enhance and build your web pages. In this tutorial, we'll create an 'Under Construction' page to show you how simple it is to use assets.

By the end of this tutorial you will be able to:

- Resize the page.

- Import and apply an asset background.

- Place and customize graphic assets.

- Place and modify button assets.

- Place and use picture frames.

- Store assets for later use.

## Let's begin...

- In the Startup Wizard, in the Create section, click **Start New Site**.

- For the purpose of this tutorial, click **Cancel**.

  This accepts the default settings and creates a new, single page site.

 We recommend that you complete the steps in the **Configure a New Site** dialog if you are starting a real site from scratch as it allows you to set up your site quickly and easily.

## Resizing the page

As we're only building a brief Under Construction page, the default web page length is too long for our purposes. Before we examine using assets, let's first adjust this page length.

### To resize the page:

1. In the workspace, right-click on the page and select **Page Properties...**

2. In the **Page Properties** dialog, select **Appearance** category, and in the **Height** input box type "650".

3. Click **OK**.

   The page will resize to 960 x 650 pixels.

 You can also resize the height (and width) of the page by dragging the page borders.

**Save now!** Click **File** > **Save As...** and choose a new name for your file.

## Using Asset Pack backgrounds

We'll start by looking at a background asset. A background asset makes it easy to add a background design to either a single page or the whole website. Its special properties ensure that it always fills the entire browser area. Before you can use an asset in your website, you need to import it into the **Assets** tab.

### To add Background assets to the Assets tab:

1.  On the **Assets** tab, click  **Browse...** to open the **Asset Browser**.

2.  In the **Categories** section, click to select the **Backgrounds** category. The backgrounds from all installed packs are displayed in the main pane.

3.  In the main pane the assets are categorized by the Pack file that they belong to. In the **Photo** pack, click on the clouds background thumbnail.

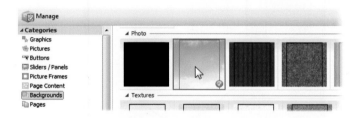

The green ⊘ shows that the asset has been added to the tab.

4. In addition, in the **Textures** pack, click on the grey marble background thumbnail.

5. Click **Close** to exit.

   Our recently imported background assets display in the **Backgrounds** category on the **Assets** tab.

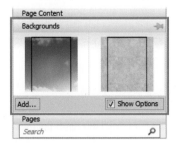

Now that we have imported the background assets, we can add one to the page.

**To add a background to the page:**

1. On the **Assets** tab, the **Backgrounds** category should be displayed (if not, click the header).

2. Drag the clouds background onto the page.

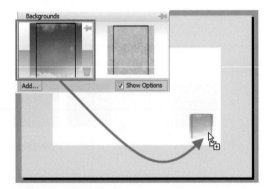

3.   In the **Apply Background Asset** dialog, ensure **Apply background asset to current page** is selected to add the background to the selected page only and click **OK**.

The background is added to the page.

Let's update the website theme by quickly changing the background.

### To change website background:

1.   On the **Assets** tab, click the **Backgrounds** category header, and drag the grey marble background onto the page.

2.   In the **Apply Background Asset** dialog, select **Apply background asset to current page**.

3.   Click **OK**.

The grey marble background instantly replaces the previously set cloud background.

If you wish to remove the background entirely:

 • For backgrounds applied to a page, click **Edit > Page Properties...** and then on the **Background** category, click **Delete All.**

 • For backgrounds applied to the entire site, click **Edit > Site Properties...** and then on the **Page > Background** category, click **Delete All.**

 Don't forget to save your work!

## Using graphic assets

Graphic assets can be used to add visual interest and give information. They are added to the **Assets** tab in exactly the same way as background assets.

### To add graphic assets to the Assets tab:

1.   On the **Assets** tab, click ☐ **Browse...** to open the **Asset Browser.**

2.   Expand the **Tags** section, and click to select the **Under Construction** tag. All assets tagged as "Under Construction" are displayed in the main pane.

3.   Click the **Add All** ◎ button for the 'Under Construction' pack. The assets are imported into the **Assets** tab.

The green ☑ shows that the asset has been added to the tab.

4. Click **Close** to exit.

## To add a graphic to the page:

1. On the **Assets** tab, the **Graphics** category should be displayed (if not, click the header).

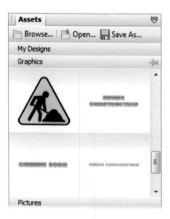

**2.**  Drag the workman sign graphic to the page.

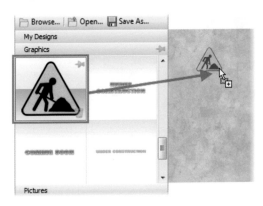

**3.**  Resize the graphic by dragging the corner handles or setting a width and height in the **Transform** tab.

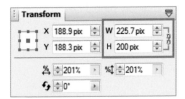

**4.**  Then use the ⊕ button to reposition it so the page looks approximately like the one illustrated below.

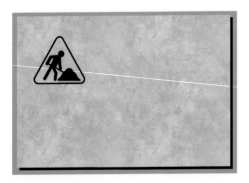

**5.** Drag the orange UNDER CONSTRUCTION text graphic to the page and then select it.

The **Hintline** toolbar at the bottom of the workspace indicates that the asset is an Artistic text object—let's customize it before we resize and position it on the page.

**6.** Click at the beginning of the Artistic text and then:

- Type "THIS PAGE IS CURRENTLY"

- Press **Shift-Return** to add a soft-return before UNDER CONSTRUCTION

- On the Text context toolbar, click ▤ **Right-align Paragraph**.

**7.** Finally, resize and reposition the Artistic text asset so that the page looks approximately like the one illustrated below.

🔺 Don't forget to save your work!

## Using Button assets

Buttons are useful tools for either triggering an event or to assist in navigating around a website. We'll add a button to our page which will allow visitors to send an email to a specified address to get more information.

### To add Button assets to the Assets tab:

1. On the **Assets** tab, click ▢ **Browse...** to open the **Asset Browser**.

2. In the **Pack Files** section, click to select the **Blank** pack in the **Website Buttons** category. All installed blank website buttons are displayed in the main pane.

3. Click the white, gradient button. The button asset is imported into the **Assets** tab.

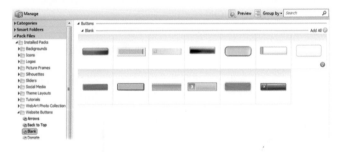

The green ⊘ shows that the asset has been added to the tab.

4. Click **Close** to exit.

## To add button to the page:

**1.** On the **Assets** tab, the **Buttons** category should be displayed (if not, click the header).

**2.** Select the button and drag it onto the page.

The button is added to the page at its default size.

Currently the button behaves like an ordinary graphic. To use it to its full potential, we need to edit some of its special properties. Next, we'll give the button a label and make it open a blank, addressed email when clicked.

## To edit button properties:

**1.** Select the button and, on the Button context toolbar, click 🖼 **Edit Button**.

**2.** In the **Edit Button** dialog, on the **Button** tab, type "Email me" in the **Button Label** box.

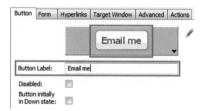

You will see the button preview update as you type.

**3.** On the **Hyperlinks** tab, click **Internet Email,** then in the **To** edit box, type your email address (e.g. me@mysite.com) or select an email address from the drop-down list.

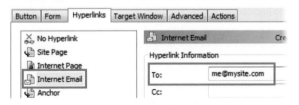

**4.** Click **OK.**

Your button will now contain the label "Email me". First we'll reposition the button and then preview the page to see the hyperlink action functioning.

**5.** With the button selected, use the  Move button to reposition the button in the top right of the page, in line with the graphic assets.

### To preview your page:

**1.** On the Standard toolbar, click the arrow to expand the 🖥️▾ **Preview site** drop-down list.

**2.** Select **Preview Page in {your web browser of choice}.**

**3.** In the browser window, click the button.

Your default, installed email client should launch and create a new email with your email address listed in the **To** addressee box.

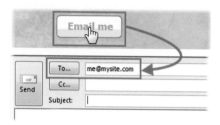

You now have a basic Under Construction page, but to add a little interest (and to give a hint at what the theme of the page is) we'll add a framed picture as a back drop. Before we do, we'll reposition the graphic assets.

### To reposition assets on the page:

**1.** Click to select the workman sign graphic and then **Shift**-click to select the Artistic text graphic. This selects both graphics simultaneously.

**2.** With both graphic assets selected, use the ⊕ button to reposition them close to the bottom of the page so that it looks approximately like the one illustrated below.

## Using Picture Frame assets

Using picture frames makes it really easy to place or swap your pictures. The tutorial, *Pictures,* on p. 65 discusses how to use blank frames. However, the installed Asset Packs contain frames with borders that can really enhance your site page. We'll add one of these now.

### To add Picture Frame assets to the Assets tab:

1. On the **Assets** tab, click 🗀 **Browse...** to open the **Asset Browser.**

2. In the **Categories** section, click to select the **Picture Frames** category. The picture frames from all installed packs are displayed in the main pane—let's slim this down using a search.

3. In the Search box, type "Rugged".

   All frames with the "Rugged" tag are displayed.

4. Click the frame with the light border. The picture frame asset is imported into the **Assets** tab.

The green 🥢 shows that the asset has been added to the tab.

5. Click **Close** to exit.

### To add a picture frame to the page:

1.  On the **Assets** tab, the **Picture Frames** category should be displayed (if not, click the header).

2.  Select the picture frame and drag it onto the page.

    The frame is added to the page at its default size.

3.  Select the frame and drag from the corner handles, or use the **Transform** tab, to resize to fill most of the page (we resized the frame to 840 x 530 pixels.

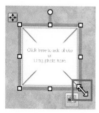

4.  Using the **Align** tab, centre the frame horizontally and vertically.

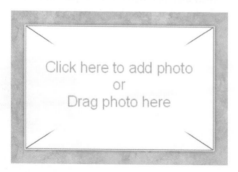

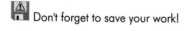 Don't forget to save your work!

We'll now add one of the installed picture assets to the frame.

### To add a picture asset to the Assets tab:

1. On the **Assets** tab, click 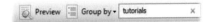 **Browse...** to open the **Asset Browser**.

2. In the **Categories** section, click to select the **Pictures** category. The images from all installed packs are displayed in the main pane.

3. In the Search box, type "tutorials".

All pictures with the "Tutorials" tag are displayed.

4. Click to select the beach umbrella and then click **Close** to exit.

### To add a picture to an existing frame:

1. On the **Assets** tab, the **Pictures** category should be displayed (if not, click the header).

2. Drag the beach umbrella thumbnail onto the picture frame. The picture is cropped to fit the frame boundary.

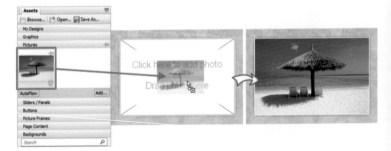

With our frame and picture added, we need to modify it to make it act as a backdrop to our page.

## To modify a picture in a frame:

1. Select the framed picture, and click  **Position Image** on the frame toolbar, and then drag on the picture to reposition it in the frame—we moved the picture upwards. (See the tutorial, *Pictures*, on p. 65 for more information.)

2. With the framed picture still selected, select the **Transparency** tab, click **Fill**, and then select the **Solid Transparency 62%** swatch.

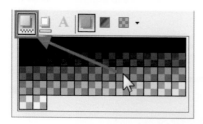

The framed picture will become semi-transparent and your previously placed assets will be visible once again.

**3.** With the framed picture still selected, on the Arrange toolbar, click  Send to Back.

That's it! So quick and simple—Assets completely transform a website. Preview your page in a browser for the full effect.

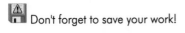 Don't forget to save your work!

### To preview your page:

**1.** On the Standard toolbar, click the arrow to expand the  Preview site drop-down list.

**2.** Select Preview Page in {your web browser of choice}.

## Storing custom designs

It can be useful to store previously modified assets and page designs for future use, on this and additional website projects. The **Assets** tab's **My Designs** category is ideal for this.

### To store individual custom designs:

1.  Select all the assets on the page (excluding the background) by clicking **Select All** from the **Edit** menu.

2.  Drag the selected items into the **My Designs** category of the **Assets** tab and release the mouse button.

Each asset is added to the **My Designs** category individually for later use. Alternatively, you can add a grouped object to the **My Designs** category as a page layout.

## To store a page layout:

*   With all the assets still selected, click  **Group Objects** on the selected objects to group them, then drag the grouped object into the **My Designs** category of the **Assets** tab.

The entire group is added as a single **Page Content** asset.

Your custom Under Construction page content asset can now be quickly and easily added to future web pages by dragging it from the **Assets** tab. Once added to the page it can be ungrouped and updated as necessary!

Why not upload your Under Construction page to the internet? See the tutorial, *Previewing & Publishing*, on p. 195 for more information.

All assets are added to the page in a similar way as described throughout this tutorial, though each asset type has its own special features once on the page. See the tutorial, *New Site from Template*, on p. 7 for details on adding **Pages** and **Page Content** assets.

# Frame Text

 15 min

To make your site as accessible as possible to everyone, you should use HTML text frames for your content. In this tutorial we'll look at the best ways of adding text to your website.

---

**WebPlus!**

Nulla vestibulum eleifend nulla. Suspendisse potenti. Aliquam turpis nisi, venenatis non, accumsan nec, imperdiet laoreet, lacus. In purus est, mattis eget, imperdiet nec, fermentum congue, tortor. Aenean ut nibh. Nullam hendrerit viverra dolor. Vestibulum fringilla, lectus id viverra malesuada, enim mi adipiscing ligula, et bibendum lacus...

---

By the end of this tutorial you will be able to:

- Create HTML text frames.

- Insert placeholder text.

- Select, edit and format text.

- Format text frames.

- Apply and edit Text Styles.

- Define HTML meta tags.

## Let's begin...

- In the Startup Wizard, in the Create section, click **Start New Site**.

- For the purpose of this tutorial, click **Cancel**.

    This accepts the default settings and creates a new, single page site.

 We recommend that you complete the steps in the **Configure a New Site** dialog if you are starting a real site from scratch as it allows you to set up your site quickly and easily.

## HTML frame text

There are two types of text in WebPlus—Artistic and HTML. Each type has different properties and they allow you to create great looking websites. However, any time you add effects such as bitmap fills, transparency, and filter effects to an artistic text object, the object is converted to a graphic when it is published. If not used carefully, this can increase the download time of your website, and prevent the use of screen readers. To stop this from happening, all main body text content should ideally be placed inside an HTML text frame.

Let's start a new site so that we have a blank canvas.

## To place an HTML text frame:

1.  On the **Quick Build** tab, in the **Layout Items** category, click the **Text Frame** layout item.

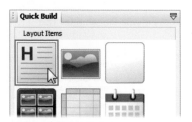

2.  With the  cursor, click and drag on the page to insert the frame at a size of your choice.

- or -

Drag the layout item thumbnail onto the page to insert the frame at its default size. (You can always resize it later.)

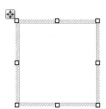

Let's now fill our frame with some text. To save time when designing a site, you can fill any text frame with placeholder text. This can help you (or your client) to visualise the overall design before the actual content is added.

## To create placeholder text:

**1.** Click inside the text frame to create an insertion point, and then type the word 'Welcome'. Press **Return** to drop to the next line.

**2.** On the **Text** menu, click **Insert > Fill with Placeholder Text**.

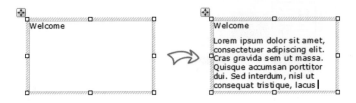

## To select, edit and format text:

**1.** Click to place an insertion point after the word 'Welcome' and press the Spacebar. Type 'to ScubaSharks!'.

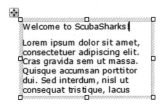

**2.** Click and drag (or triple-click) on the first line of text to select it.

**3.** On the Text context toolbar, in the styles drop-down list, select **Heading 1**. The heading is updated.

**4.** After step 3, you might find that the text no longer fits. You may also see an  Overflow button.

This means that there is more text in the frame than can fit at one time. However, it's easy to resize a frame without changing the appearance of the text within. Let's do this now.

### To resize a frame by dragging:

**1.** Move the mouse pointer over the frame's right-centre handle. The pointer will change to a double-headed arrow.

**2.** Click and drag to resize the frame so that it stretches across the page, leaving some extra space for additional text.

The actual text formatting doesn't change, it simply re-aligns to fit within the boundaries of the frame.

Let's add another heading to our text frame. This time, we'll format it using the **Heading 2** text style.

## To format text using text styles:

1.  Click inside the text frame to create an insertion point at the end of the existing text, and then press **Return** to drop to the next line. Type the words 'PADI Scuba courses'.

2.  On the Text context toolbar, in the styles drop-down list, select **Heading 2**.

The style is applied to the text.

When you resize an HTML text frame, you are only resizing the text container. The formatting of the text will not change. However, resizing an Artistic text object once it is placed on the page will change the formatting of the text itself. Artistic text that is stretched or squashed will always be output as a graphic.

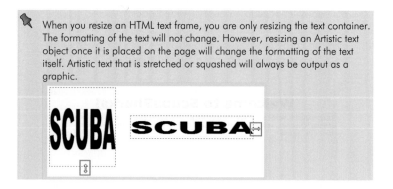

## To select, copy and paste text:

1.  Triple-click on the paragraph in the text frame. The entire paragraph is selected.

2.  On the Standard toolbar, click **Copy** (or press **Ctrl + C**).

3.    Click next to the word 'courses' and press **Enter** to create a new line.

4.    Click **Paste** (or press **Ctrl + V**). The text is inserted.

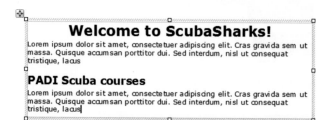

   Changing the font

> You can choose any font you like for your HTML text, but we recommend selecting from the **Fonts** tab's Websafe list for best possible results.

   Don't forget to save your work!

## Formatting Text Frames

If you want to make your text stand out from other text on your pages, why not format the text frame so that it creates an attractive container. Over the next few steps we'll apply a fill and padding to the text frame.

### To change the fill colour of a text frame:

1.    Click the text frame border to select the text frame (the border will turn to a solid outline).

2.    On the Swatches tab, click the  **Fill** button and then click a colour swatch to apply it. We selected Scheme Colour 2.

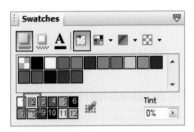

The fill is applied to your frame.

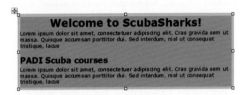

As you can see, the text goes right up to the edges of the frame. Now that we've added colour this doesn't look as good. We can improve things dramatically by adding some internal padding to the frame.

### To add internal padding:

1. Ensure that the text frame is selected and on the Text context toolbar, click 🖻 **Frame Setup**.

2. In the dialog, set the all four margins to 10 pix and click **OK**.

   The frame is updated.

3. (Optional) If necessary, resize the container to fit the text.

## Text Styles

By using text styles, it makes it easy to keep the formatting of your text consistent.

We'll illustrate this by changing the text colour.

### To update a text style:

1.   (Optional) Click or hover over the ‖ handle (near the Web Objects toolbar) to display the tabs on the left.

2.   Click the **Text Styles** tab.

3.   Move the mouse pointer over the **Normal** style and click the down-arrow. (If a style is not displayed, select 🖼 **Show All** at the top of the **Text Styles** tab.)

4.   Click **Modify Normal...**

5.   In the **Text Style** dialog:

     •   In the left pane, in the **Character** category, click the **Font** sub-category.

- Click to expand the **Text fill** drop-down list and then click the Scheme Colour 11 swatch.

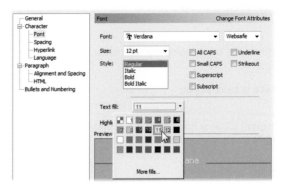

- Click **OK**.

**6.** All of the body text in the frame is updated with the new colour!

 By default, most styles are based on the **Normal** text style, so, by modifying Normal, the change is reflected throughout all of the Text Styles (and therefore your site). This makes it easy to quickly change the font, size and colour of your entire site.

 Don't forget to save your work!

We couldn't finish this tutorial without looking at the main advantage of using HTML text frames—HTML meta tags. These are used by search engines to categorize your site. If you assign a meta tag to a text style, WebPlus will automatically generate the code when the site is published.

Let's do this now.

**To apply an HTML meta tag to a style:**

1.   On the **Text Styles** tab, move the mouse pointer over the **Heading 1** style and click the down-arrow.

2.   Click **Modify Heading 1...**

3.   In the **Text Style** dialog:

     •   In the left pane, in the **Paragraph** category, click the **HTML** sub-category.

     •   Select the appropriate HTML tag (in this case **H1** is already selected).

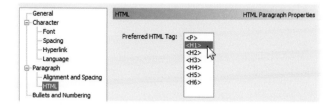

     •   Click **OK**.

         The **H1** tag will be applied whenever the **Heading 1** style is used within an HTML text frame.

The **Text Styles** tab contains preset Heading styles which translate to HTML tags **H1** to **H6**. You can format the text style to suit your site design while keeping those important tags. For more information on modifying text styles see WebPlus Help.

We've covered many useful tips for creating, editing, and managing text with WebPlus. We hope that you're now feeling more comfortable with the different text objects we've described and are ready to get started creating content for your own site! If you haven't done so already, you may want to have a look at the online tutorial, *Artistic text*.

# Pictures

30 min

Using pictures is a great way to create an eye-catching website. However, used incorrectly, they can slow the loading of your site and frustrate visitors. WebPlus has a few tricks for placing pictures while optimizing page download. We'll introduce you to these tricks for importing, placing, and managing pictures on your website.

By the end of this tutorial you will be able to:

- Use picture frames.

- Adjust pictures in frames.

- Use pictures from the Assets tab.

- Import and place pictures on the page.

- Create self-linking picture hyperlinks.

- Apply various picture effects.

- Modify global and individual image format settings.

- Add ALT and TITLE text to pictures.

## Let's begin...

1.    On the **File** menu, click **Startup Wizard...**

2.    In the Create section, click **Use Design Template**.

3.    In the dialog:

- In the **Theme Layouts** list on the left, select the **Nature** layout.

- At the bottom, click ⊞ **Deselect All**.

- In the right **Pages** pane, select **Home** only.

4.    Click **Open**.

The layout opens in the workspace.

This theme layout page provides several picture frames waiting to accommodate your pictures.

## Using picture frames

Placing picture frames on your site pages has several benefits:

- You can use empty frames as 'placeholder' areas when you know you want to add pictures, but have yet to put them in, as in WebPlus theme layouts.

- Frames make it easy to place pictures at a specific size or shape, without changing the aspect ratio—useful for 'contact' pictures or thumbnails.

- You can easily swap the pictures displayed inside frames without altering the page layout.

You can add pictures individually by clicking directly on a picture frame, or you can add multiple pictures to the **Assets** tab and then drag them onto the frames as you need them. We'll demonstrate both methods. We'll be using the sample pictures installed with WebPlus. However, you can use your own pictures if you prefer.

### To add a picture to a frame:

1. Select the top-left picture frame and then click 🖼 **Replace Picture**.

   - or -

   Click inside the top-left picture frame.

2. In the **Import Picture** dialog, browse to your **Images** folder.

 In a standard installation, the Images folder is found in **C:\Program Files\Serif\WebPlus\X6\Images**. However, the path may differ if you are running a 64 bit operating system or if you changed the installation location.

**3.**   Select the picture of the white house (4504276.jpg) and click **Open**.

**4.**   The picture is added to the frame and scaled to maximum-fit by default.

When the picture is selected, note that the Picture Frame toolbar displays in the lower-right corner. You can use these tools to adjust your picture inside the frame.

## To adjust a picture inside a frame:

* To reposition the picture inside the frame, click  **Pan**, and then click and drag on the picture with the ⌐ **Pan** cursor.

* To rotate the picture in 90° increments, click ⬛ **Rotate Left** or ⬛ **Rotate Right**.

* To zoom in or out of the picture in increments, click ⬛ **Zoom In** or ⬛ **Zoom Out**.

* To replace the picture, click ⬛ **Replace Picture**, browse to and select a new picture and click **Open**.

* To change the scale options, on the Picture context toolbar, click ⬛ **Frame Properties** and change the option in the dialog.

## Using the Assets tab

WebPlus provides a selection of royalty-free pictures for you to use in your website. These can be quickly imported and conveniently stored in the **Assets** tab for easy access and quick addition to your site.

 We've provided a convenient **Tutorial** asset pack which contains all the pictures you will need to help you progress through WebPlus tutorials.

### To add Picture assets to the Assets tab:

1.  On the **Assets** tab, click 🗀 **Browse...** to open the **Asset Browser**.

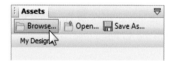

2.  In the **Categories** section, click to select the **Pictures** category. The pictures from all installed packs are displayed in the main pane.

3.  In the main pane the assets are categorized by the Pack file that they belong to. In the **Tutorials** pack, click on the beach umbrella thumbnail.

The green 🅐 shows that the asset has been added to the tab.

4.  Click **Close** to exit.

Our recently imported picture asset displays in the **Pictures** category on the **Assets** tab.

Now that we have imported a picture asset, we can add it to a picture frame.

### To add a picture to a frame using the Assets tab:

1.  On the **Assets** tab, the **Pictures** category should be displayed (if not, click the header).

2.  Drag the picture onto the top-right picture frame.

You can populate all the empty picture frames in your website with one click from the **Assets** tab!

With multiple pictures imported into the **Pictures** category, simply click **AutoFlow**.

You might prefer to add your own pictures to the **Assets** tab before adding them to your site.

### To add your own pictures to the Asset tab:

1.   On the **Assets** tab, click the **Pictures** category header and then click the **Add...** button.

2.   In the **Import Picture** dialog, browse to the folder which contains your pictures and then select the pictures you want to import. (Use **Ctrl**- and **Shift**-click to select multiple pictures.)

3.   Click **Open**.

     Your pictures are imported directly into the **Assets** tab for use in your current website.

 Don't forget to save your work!

## Adding picture frames

If you're designing a page (or site) from scratch you may wish to add picture frames to your page for the reasons highlighted above. Let's do that now...

**To add a new blank page:**

1. On the **Site** tab, click the arrow on the ⊞ ⁻ **Add new page or link** drop-down list and select **New Blank Page...**

2. In the **Page Properties** dialog, click **OK**.

A new page displays in the workspace.

**To add a picture frame to the page:**

1. On the **Quick Build** tab, in the **Layout Items** category, **Ctrl**-click the **Picture** layout item.

2. With the ⁺▣ cursor, click and drag on the page to pre-define the picture frame size.

Alternatively, for a picture frame set to the default size:

• On the **Quick Build** tab, in the **Layout Items** category, **Ctrl**-drag the **Picture** layout item to the page.

You can now populate the picture frame by double-clicking inside the frame, by clicking ▣ **Replace Picture**, or dragging pictures from the **Assets** tab (as previously discussed).

## Adding pictures directly to a page

Although picture frames can be useful in building and updating a site, you can also add pictures directly to a page, without using picture frames.

You can add pictures individually by using the **Import Picture** tool, or you can add multiple pictures to the **Assets** tab and then drag them onto your page as you need them. We'll demonstrate both methods.

### To add a picture directly to the page:

1.  On the **Quick Build** tab, in the **Layout Items** category, click the **Picture** layout item.

2.  With the ⁺▣ cursor, click and drag on the page to pre-define a thumbnail picture size.

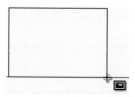

3.  In the **Import Picture** dialog, browse to your **Images** folder.

4.  Select the beach umbrella (4569785.jpg) and click **Open**.

You can scale a picture at any time by selecting it and dragging its handles.

### To add pictures using the Asset tab:

- On the **Assets** tab, click the **Pictures** category header, and then drag a picture onto the page.

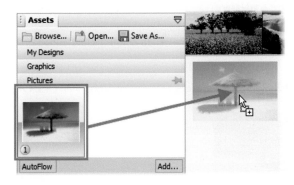

The picture is added at its native size—you can resize this to fit neatly on the page.

## Applying adjustments and effects

Now let's move on and discuss a few more hints and tips for enhancing your pictures...

### To add transparency effects:

1.  With the picture selected, click the **Transparency** tab and expand the **Bitmap** drop-down list.

2.  Click to display the **Photo Edge Effects** category and then click the **Bitmap Transparency 25** swatch.

## To recolour a picture:

1.  Select the picture and click the Re-colour Picture button on the Picture context toolbar.

2.  In the **Fill** dialog, click a black colour swatch and then click **OK**.

3.  Try experimenting with other colours, for example, create a sepia tone effect by applying a brown or dark orange fill colour, or use a scheme colour (as we have in our example). See the online tutorial, *Colour Schemes*, for more information on using colour schemes.

## To apply a picture adjustment:

•   With the picture selected, on the Picture context toolbar, click a **Contrast**, **Brightness**, or **Tonal Range** adjustment and repeat as required.

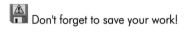 Don't forget to save your work!

## ALT & TITLE text

ALT and TITLE text is important to use to ensure that your website is accessible to everyone.

- TITLE text is the tooltip text that will appear when site visitors hover over the picture in their Web browsers. This text is often used when clicking on a picture has some function, for example, opening a larger version of the picture in a new window (see the tutorial *Creating Hyperlinks & Anchors* on p. 79 for more information on how to create these).

- ALT text, used to describe the content and/or purpose of a picture, is the text that will appear in the area of your page where the picture will download. (Note that ALT text should *not* be used for pictures whose only purpose is decorative.)

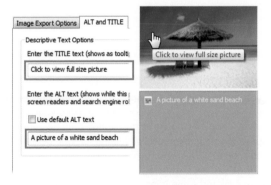

### To set ALT and TITLE text for a picture:

1.  Right-click on a picture and choose **Export Options...**

2.  In the dialog, on the **ALT and TITLE** tab, enter TITLE and ALT text.

By default, the **Use default ALT text** option is selected. This tells WebPlus to use the TITLE text as the ALT description so that you only have to enter it once. By clearing the check box (as we have done) you can have different ALT and TITLE text. You can also choose to only have ALT text.

In order to accurately reproduce your design as a Web page, it is possible that items you create in WebPlus will be published as images. To allow for this, ALT and TITLE options are available for regular WebPlus objects as well as for imported pictures.

WebPlus will attempt to create ALT text for any text that is exported as a graphic.

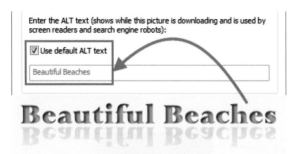

For more information, see *Setting Picture Export Options* in WebPlus Help.

We suggest that you experiment with ALT and TITLE text and preview your results. ALT text is an important consideration when making your site accessible to as many people as possible, and it may even help improve your site's rankings in search engine results. See the tutorial, *Search Engine Optimization*, on p. 209 for more information.

In this tutorial, we've explored some image import options, some efficiency and quality issues, and some publishing considerations. See the online tutorial, *Managing Your Web Presence*, for more information.

# Creating Hyperlinks & Anchors

 30 min

WebPlus provides a wide and very flexible range of hyperlink options. This means easy navigation for your site's visitors—and possibly a more efficient visit if your site includes large pictures.

By the end of this tutorial you will be able to:

* Create anchors.

* Create a hyperlink to an anchor.

* Create a 'to top' hyperlink.

* Create self-linking picture hyperlinks.

* Create a link to a site page.

* Create external hyperlinks.

 Go to **http://go.serif.com/resources/WPX6** to download the following tutorial project file(s):

 portfolio.wpp

## Let's begin...

1. On the Standard toolbar, click  **Open**.

2. Navigate to your website file, select it and click **Open**.

   The 'Home' page is displayed in the workspace.

**Save now!** Click **File > Save As...** and choose a new name for your file.

## Introducing anchors and hyperlinks

Hyperlinks are an effective way of navigating around websites—when using the internet, you'll frequently use hyperlinks, perhaps even subconsciously.

Almost any object on your page can have a hyperlink assigned to it or can be the destination for a hyperlink. We'll explore the two most frequent examples—text and pictures.

We'll add some anchors and hyperlinks to the **Illustration portfolio** site.

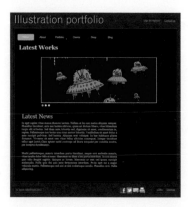

Let's first look at setting up some page anchors.

## Adding anchors

Anchors act as fixed points on your site which you can link to—anchors are used if you wish to direct visitors to a single point on a page rather than the entire page. Anchors must be created first before a hyperlink can established to it.

Let's imagine there is a sale on 'The Humans Are Coming' print listed on the 'Shop' page. We want to highlight this fact on the 'Home' page and provide a direct link to the item on sale.

First we need to add an anchor to the sale item...

### To add an anchor:

1.    On the **Site** tab, double-click the **Shop** page.

      The Shop page will be displayed in your workspace.

2. Use the ⬉ **Pointer tool** to place an insertion point at the beginning of the text box next to the bottom picture—in our example, the words 'The Humans Are Coming'.

- or -

Use the ⬉ **Pointer tool** to select the bottom picture.

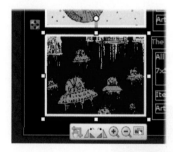

3. On the **Format** menu, click **Anchor...**

- or -

On the Web Properties toolbar, click ⓘ **Anchor.**

4. In the **Anchor** dialog box, type 'TheHumansAreComing' and then click **OK**. (Note that anchor names cannot contain spaces.)

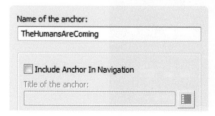

Anchors can be added to any object on any page, so it's possible to create unique navigation, and to offer speedy access to any of your site's content.

Anchors for important parts of your site can be included within navigation bars by checking the **Include Anchor In Navigation** option. (In these cases, make sure that you give the anchor a meaningful title as this is what your site visitors will see.) See the tutorial, *Navigation bars,* on p. 95 for more information.

 Why not add a sale sticker to the page using content from the **Assets** tab?

See the tutorial, *Assets,* on p. 33 for more details.

## Linking to anchors

We now have an anchor which specifically identifies the sale item on the 'Shop' page. But how do we make use of this anchor?

To make the best use of an anchor, we need to create a hyperlink to take visitors to it!

### To link to an anchor:

1.  On the **Site** tab, double-click the **Home** page.

    The 'Home' page will be displayed in your workspace.

2.  Use the ↖ **Pointer tool** to highlight the second paragraph in the text frame and press the **Delete** key.

3.  On the Frame text context toolbar, in the **Style** drop-down list, click **Heading 2**, and then click ≣ **Align Centre**.

    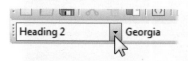

4.  Type 'Sale on selected prints!' and then drag with the ↖ **Pointer tool** to select the text.

5.  On the **Format** menu, click **Hyperlink...**

    - or -

    On the Web Properties toolbar, click 🖼 **Hyperlink**.

**6.** In the **Edit Hyperlink** dialog:

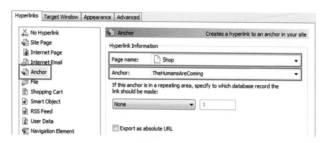

- Choose the **Anchor** category.

- In the **Page name** drop-down list, select **Shop**.

- In the **Anchor** drop-down list, select **TheHumansAreComing**.

- Click **OK**.

 The **Export as absolute URL** option lets your site visitors add your page as a bookmark. This is especially important if you use frames to display content within your site.

The text now has a hyperlink attached to it.

 Don't forget to save your work!

## Previewing your hyperlink

You now have a hyperlink to an anchor on a separate page, let's see how it works!

### To preview a site:

1.  On the Standard toolbar, click the arrow to expand the  **Preview site** drop-down list.

2.  Select **Preview Site in {your web browser of choice}**.

3.  Hover over the hyperlink and you will see the cursor change to the 🖐 hand cursor.

4.  Click on the link and the 'Shop' page will display with 'The Humans Are Coming' in full view.

As you can see, the top of the page is not visible—this page is particularly long. Currently, to return to the top of the page, a visitor needs to scroll back up. Let's help our visitors by setting up a shortcut for returning to the top of the page.

## Creating 'to top' hyperlinks

For long web pages you may want to offer a link back to the top of the page. WebPlus automatically creates a 'top' anchor for every web page in your site, all you need to do is simply link text or images to this pre-defined 'top' anchor!

### To create a 'top' link:

1.  On the **Site** tab, double-click the **Shop** page.

    The 'Shop' page will be displayed in your workspace.

2.  On the Drawing toolbar, click $\mathbf{A}$ **Artistic Text**.

3.  Click at the bottom-right of the page to add a text object with default formatting.

4.  Type 'Top of page' and then drag with the ⬉ **Pointer tool** to select the text.

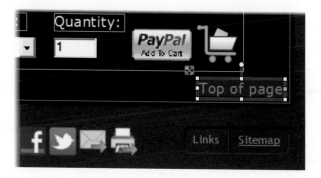

5.  On the **Format** menu, click **Hyperlink...**

**6.** In the **Edit Hyperlink** dialog:

- Choose the **Anchor** category.

- In the **Anchor** drop-down list, select **top**.

- Click **OK**.

Feel free to preview your site, as mentioned on p. 86, to see the hyperlink in action.

 A 'top' link can also be added to a graphic or picture by selecting it and then follow steps 5 and 6 above.

## Linking to pictures

We've just examined how to jump to specific points on a page, but hyperlinks can perform other tasks too. In the next section, we'll show you how to link to a larger version of a picture. This is useful if you want to show visitors a quick-loading, small thumbnail picture but also allow them to access and download a larger, high resolution copy of the same picture.

### To create a 'self-linking' picture:

1.  Use the ▶ **Pointer tool** to select a picture—in our example, the 'City' picture on the 'Shop' page.

2.  Right-click the picture and click **Hyperlink...**

3.  In the **Edit Hyperlink and Actions** dialog:

    *   On the **Hyperlinks** tab, choose the **Picture** category.

    *   On the **Target Window** tab, from the **Type** drop-down list, choose **New Window**.

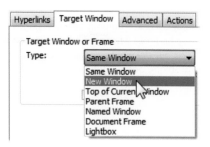

    *   Click **OK**.

Feel free to preview your site, as mentioned on p. 86, to see the hyperlink in action.

Don't forget to save your work!

## Creating a link to a site page

Navigation bars are generally used for jumping between pages within a website. However, there may be times when you have excluded pages from the main navigation bar but still want visitors to access them easily. A hyperlink can solve this problem. See the tutorial, *Navigation bars*, on p. 95 for more information on navigation bars.

In our **Illustration portfolio** example, you can see that the 'Links' page has been excluded from the main navigation bar.

Let's create a hyperlink to the 'Links' page and add a little flair by opening it in a lightbox.

### To create a link to a site page:

1. On the **Site** tab, expand the **Master Pages** section, and then double-click on **Master A**.

   Master page A will display in the workspace.

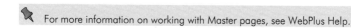 For more information on working with Master pages, see WebPlus Help.

2. Use the ▶ **Pointer tool** to select the 'links' text in the bottom, right-hand corner of the page.

3. On the **Format** menu, click **Hyperlink...**

4. In the **Edit Hyperlink** dialog:

   • On the **Hyperlinks** tab, choose the **Site Page** category.

- Select **Links** from the **Page name** drop-down list.

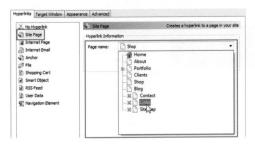

- On the **Target Window** tab, in the **Type** drop-down list, choose **Lightbox**.

- Click **OK**.

Feel free to preview your site, as mentioned on p. 86, to see the hyperlink in action.

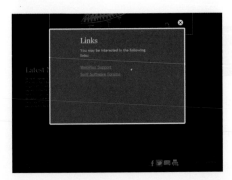

## Creating an external hyperlink

For this final section, we'll look at setting up a hyperlink on the 'About' page which links to an external website on the internet—the procedure is very similar to what we've previously explored throughout this tutorial.

### To create an external hyperlink:

1.   On the **Site** tab, double-click the **About** page.

     The 'About' page will be displayed in your workspace.

2.   Right-click one of the graphics under the sketch, and then click **Hyperlink...**

3.   In the **Edit Hyperlink and Actions** dialog:

     •   On the **Hyperlinks** tab, choose the **Internet Page** category.

     •   Type in the URL for the external site in the **URL address** box or click a previously entered URL from the drop-down list.

     •   On the **Target Window** tab, in the **Type** drop-down list, choose **New Window** and then click **OK**.

Whenever linking to an external website, we recommend setting the target window or frame to **New Window**, this way your visitor will not lose access to your website—it will still be open in their browser.

 Don't forget to save your work!

Feel free to preview your site, as mentioned on p. 86, to see the hyperlink in action.

Congratulations! You've come to the end of the tutorial and the **Illustration portfolio** site is now full of hyperlinks to help your visitors navigate around. We'll leave you to add more links and explore the other hyperlink types listed in the **Hyperlinks** dialog—most are self-explanatory in their nature.

 Hyperlinks can have a big impact on getting your website noticed by search engines. See the tutorial, *Search Engine Optimization*, on p. 209 for more information.

 Hyperlinks and anchors can be viewed and managed from the **Site Manager**, which you can access from the context toolbar.

For more information on using **Site Manager**, see WebPlus Help.

# Navigation Bars

 15-20 min

Having fantastic content on your website is useless unless your visitors can get to it! Navigation bars are essential to successful site navigation. Luckily for us, WebPlus has a whole host of professionally designed dynamic navigation bars for us to use, and the process is easy.

By the end of this tutorial you will be able to:

* Change the design of an existing navigation bar.

* Customize a navigation bar.

* Use Child and Same Level navigation bars.

* Insert a site map.

 If you're unfamiliar with website structure, we suggest you review the basic concepts before beginning this tutorial. See WebPlus Help or the tutorial, *Understanding Site Structure*, on p. 23.

## Let's begin...

1.   On the **File** menu, click **Startup Wizard...**

2.   In the Create section, click **Use Design Template**.

3.   In the dialog:

     •    In the **Theme Layouts** list on the left, click **Doodle**.

     •    Click **Open**.

          The page opens in the workspace.

## Changing the style of an existing navigation bar

Notice that this template already contains a navigation bar.

Generally, the main 'top level' navigation bar is shared by all of the
pages on a website. As a result, the navigation bar is usually placed on
the underlying master page. This means that you only have to place the
navigation bar once, even though it appears on each page. The bar on
this layout is very small so let's update it to something a little different.

## To change the navigation bar design:

1. Click to select the existing navigation bar and then click  **Edit on Master Page**.

The master page is displayed in the workspace.

2. Double-click the navigation bar to open the **Navigation Bar Settings** dialog.

3. In the dialog, click to display the **Type** tab.

   The category list (highlighted red) displays the available navigation bar categories. A preview is displayed in the main pane (highlighted blue).

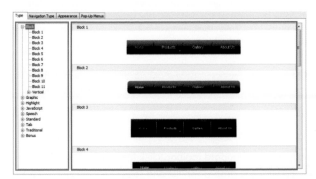

4. Click on a category item to view a preview of the bar. (If you point to a part of the bar containing a pop-up menu the menu will also preview.)

We selected the Block 9 navigation bar style.

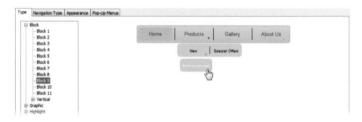

5.  For now we'll accept the default appearance. Click **OK** to exit.

    The navigation bar is updated on the page.

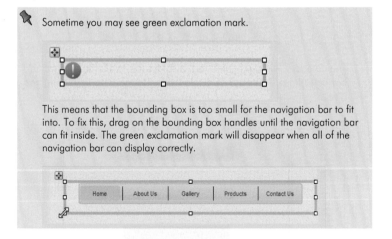

Sometime you may see green exclamation mark.

This means that the bounding box is too small for the navigation bar to fit into. To fix this, drag on the bounding box handles until the navigation bar can fit inside. The green exclamation mark will disappear when all of the navigation bar can display correctly.

6.  Finally, on the Standard toolbar, click the arrow to expand the ⬚▾ **Preview site** drop-down list and select **Preview Site in {your web browser of choice}**.

    Your site will open in a new browser window. Notice that the navigation bar has updated throughout the site, even though we only changed it once, This is because it is placed on the master page.

Many of the navigation bars have been created to use scheme colours and will update when placed on the page to match the current scheme. See the online tutorial, *Colour Schemes*, for more information on using colour schemes.

## Customizing a navigation bar

Now let's customize one of the pre-designed navigation bars.

### To customize the navigation buttons:

1. Double-click the navigation bar to open the **Navigation Bar Settings** dialog.

2. Click to display the **Appearance** tab. Notice that a dynamic preview of the navigation bar displays at the bottom of the dialog.

Here you can change the style of the buttons, separators and background. You can even create your own design from scratch! This would be a tutorial in itself, so for now, we'll just change the style of the buttons to one of the pre-designed ones.

**3.** Click the arrow next to the **Single** button. A drop-down list of all available buttons is displayed. Click to select a different button. We decided on one of the buttons in the **Traditional** category.

The preview updates to show your new button in place.

**4.** To preview your navigation bar on a different 'page' background colour, select a different swatch from the **Preview Background** drop-down palette. This will help you to decide whether your navigation bar will fit in with your site background.

**5.** When you're happy with your changes, click **OK**.

**6.** Click **Preview Site in {your browser of choice}** to see your new navigation bar in action.

Buttons, backgrounds and separators are created using images with special properties.

If you want to be more adventurous with your navigation bar or button design, click on the  Edit button. This will take you into the appropriate design studio. You'll find detailed information on using the design tools in the studio **How To** pane.

 The **portfolio.wpp** example file that is used throughout the tutorials uses a customized navigation bar from the **Standard** category.

## Other types of navigation

In most websites, the main navigation bar is kept fairly simple, showing only the main, top-level pages of the website. However, it is not uncommon to have several types of navigation bar used throughout your website. WebPlus makes this process very easy—it is even possible to maintain a consistent look throughout by sharing navigation bar styles between navigation bars. We don't have time to go into that now, but you can find out more about this in WebPlus Help.

We'll conclude this tutorial by looking at a few examples from a completed version of our portfolio website. However, we won't go into step-by-step detail—the general formatting process is much the same as the steps we followed to create our top-level navigation earlier in the tutorial.

If you want to look at our examples in action, you'll need a copy of the **portfolio.wpp** file. If you haven't already downloaded it, you can do so now.

 Go to **http://go.serif.com/resources/WPX6** to download the following tutorial project file(s):

 portfolio.wpp

## Same Level navigation bar

Each of the portfolio gallery pages has a **Same Level** navigation bar. This makes it easy for the visitor to jump between these child pages, without having to use the drop-down list off the main navigation bar. It also makes it obvious at a glance that there is more to explore.

The bar itself has been added as a single object to a new **Master B** page which is assigned to the child pages in addition to the main master page, **Master B**.

You can assign multiple master pages in the **Site** tab by simply dragging additional master pages onto the page entry. A ⊞ is displayed on the entry to signify that it now uses more than one master page.

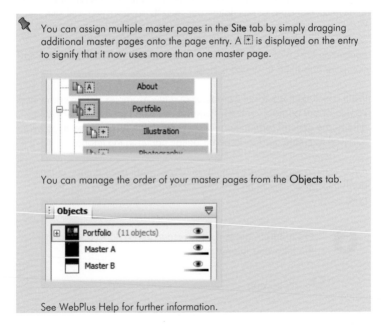

You can manage the order of your master pages from the **Objects** tab.

See WebPlus Help for further information.

If you want to follow the steps below in the **portfolio.wpp** file, you will need to delete the existing navigation bar from the **Master B** master page.

### To add a Same Level navigation element:

1.  Ensure that the page to which you want to add the navigation bar (Master B in our example **portfolio.wpp** file) is displayed in the workspace.

2.  Drag the **Navigation Bar** element from the **Quick Build** tab to your page.

3.  The **Navigation Bar Settings** dialog opens:

    *   Choose a navigation bar design from one of the categories (we chose Standard 10).

    *   On the **Navigation Type** tab, click **Same Level**.

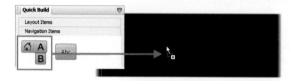

    *   If required you can modify appearance and pop-up menus in the relevant tabs.

4.  Click **OK** to accept changes and exit the dialog.

5. (Optional) Drag the navigation bar into position on the page and resize it so that it spans most of the page.

6. (Optional) If the navigation bar is displayed at the bottom of the page, on the right-click menu, click **Arrange** > **Attach to Bottom of Page**.

Now when you preview the site, the navigation bar on the child pages will show all of the pages at the same level.

## Child Level navigation bar

On our website we have a **Top Level**, 'Portfolio' page which contains three child pages. We wanted a navigation bar to display the child pages. To keep the navigation consistent, we applied the **Master B** master page containing the navigation bar. However, this caused the navigation to show the wrong pages as it was set to **Same Level** navigation. To fix this, we needed to change it to **Child Level**.

Rather than create an entire new master page, we simply use 🗟 **Promote from Master Page** to create a special instance of the navigation bar, and then change the navigation settings to display **Child Level** pages.

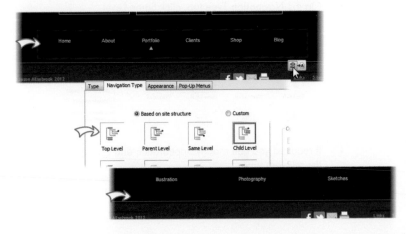

This form of navigation allows the visitor to get to relevant pages on the site, without delving through menus. It also makes it plainly obvious that there is more content to see.

## Sitemaps

Our final navigation example is a site map. This is a special type of navigation element that displays every page in your site. It allows visitors to jump straight to any page and can help to elevate your site's status within search engines.

Normally, a site map is placed on a page that is not included within any of the navigation bars. (This is shown by a grey page entry in the **Site** tab.) Instead, a simple link is provided to it on the master page. However, smaller sites may place a sitemap at the bottom of a master page.

### To add a Sitemap navigation element:

1.  In the **Site** tab, double click on the 'Sitemap' page to display it in the workspace.

2.  At the bottom of the workspace, drag the **Navigation Bar** element from the **Quick Build** tab to your page.

**3.** The **Navigation Bar Settings** dialog opens:

- In the left-most category list, expand the **Javascript** and select **Site Map**. The navigation element is displayed in the preview pane. Select one of the available designs.

- On the **Navigation Type** tab, ensure that the **Include anchors** check box is selected if you have used anchors in your site.

- If required you can set advanced options and change the appearance in the **Options** and **Style** tabs.

**4.** When you're finished, click **OK**. The sitemap is placed on the page.

Well, that concludes this tutorial. We hope this exercise has convinced you of the versatility of navigation bars that not only adapt to your site structure but blend harmoniously with your site's visual design.

Equipped with a basic knowledge of these remarkable WebPlus features, you're ready to create your own website layouts. Now it's up to you and your imagination!

# Photo Galleries

 15-20 min

With WebPlus, you can add stunning photo galleries to your websites. Simply add your photos, and then choose from a range of professionally-designed templates. You can customize the templates to suit the theme of your photos, and even add background music!

By the end of this tutorial you will be able to:

- Create a photo gallery.

- Add photos to a photo gallery.

- Organize photos within a photo gallery.

- Add captions to photos.

- Apply gallery styles and settings.

- Edit an existing photo gallery.

- Add hyperlinks to photos.

## Let's begin...

* In the Startup Wizard, in the Create section, click **Start New Site**.

* For the purpose of this tutorial, click **Cancel**.

  This accepts the default settings and creates a new, single page site.

 We recommend that you complete the steps in the **Configure a New Site** dialog if you are starting a real site from scratch as it allows you to set up your site quickly and easily.

## Types of photo gallery

WebPlus offers four types of photo gallery, each with their own unique set of features—here's a brief overview to help you decide which gallery best suits your needs.

Professional Flash™, Professional Flash™ (Live Feed), Flash™ and JavaScript photo galleries each offer different gallery styles and user navigation settings.

Professional Flash is more suitable for displaying large photo collections—you can present your photos in multiple albums. It offers horizontal thumbnail rollover styles which enable you to define basic preferences, as well as settings for captions, navigation bars, albums and hyperlinks. By enabling advanced options you can also define your preferences for gallery transitions, timers, and text.

Professional Flash (Live Feed) works as described above but you can load images into the gallery from an RSS 2.0 Media feed or SlideShowPro

Director content system. Your gallery is automatically updated when you add more photos to your Media feed or content system. Also you can export your preferred gallery settings to file so that you can import them to use whenever you create a Professional Flash gallery.

**Flash** is ideal for displaying smaller photo collections and **JavaScript** is a suitable alternative to using Flash™ on your site. They both offer horizontal and vertical thumbnail rollover, photo grid and photo stack styles. You can define settings for gallery position, thumbnails, navigation bars, captions and transitions. With Flash only, you can also add background music.

## Creating a photo gallery

For this exercise, you'll need a selection of your own photographs or pictures, perhaps choosing ones which fit well with your website theme. We'll create a photo gallery using photographs taken on a visit to a falconry centre and place this on a new blank website, but you may want to add yours to an existing WebPlus project.

 For information on creating a photo gallery using online content, i.e. a **Live Feed** gallery, see WebPlus Help.

### To add a photo gallery to the page:

1.  On the **Quick Build** tab, in the **Layout Items** category, click the **Photo Gallery** layout item.

2. With the  cursor, click and drag on the page to pre-define the photo gallery size.

   - or -

• For a photo gallery set to the default size:

   On the **Quick Build** tab, in the **Layout Items** category, drag the **Photo Gallery** layout item to the page.

Following either insertion method, the **Photo Gallery** dialog opens.

### To create a photo gallery:

1. In the **Photo Gallery** dialog, select the type of gallery you want to use:

   • Professional Flash Photo Gallery

   • Flash Photo Gallery

   • JavaScript Gallery

   The procedure for adding a photo gallery to your site is the same for all three types of gallery. For this exercise, we've selected a **Professional Flash Photo Gallery**.

Can't decide which type of gallery to choose? See our Types of photo gallery overview on p. 108.

2. Click **Next**.

## Adding and organizing your photos

The second window in the Photo Gallery dialog allows you to add and organize your gallery photos.

### To add photos to a photo gallery:

1.  In the **Photo Gallery** dialog, click 📷 **Add Folder**.

2.  In the **Browse For Folder** dialog, select the folder containing your photos and click **OK**.

    Your photos display as thumbnails in the dialog.

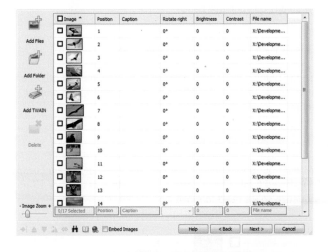

3.  The buttons running down the left side of the dialog offer the following options:

    -   📷 **Add Files:** Choose this option to add individual photos to your gallery.

- **Add Folder:** Choose this option to add photos contained inside a folder on your computer.

- **Add TWAIN:** Choose this option to add photos from a TWAIN source, such as a scanner or digital camera. (For details, see WebPlus Help.)

- **Delete:** Choose this option to delete selected photos that you no longer want in your gallery.

With all the photographs now added, we can organize and edit them to help the gallery content flow better.

### To organize photos within the gallery:

1. Use the buttons across the lower edge of the dialog to adjust image order, rotate images, edit albums, edit hyperlinks, and embed images.

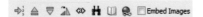

   We want our photo gallery to begin with the photo of the European Long-Eared Eagle Owl. Currently this photo is at number 13 in the sequence so we need to move it.

**2.**  Select the photo check box and then click 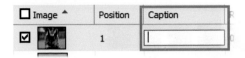 **Move to position**.

In the **Move To** dialog, input the number 1 and then click OK, to move the photo to first place in the sequence.

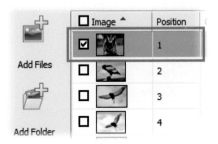

If you need to, zoom into your images using the **Image Zoom** slider.

**3.**  (Optional) To embed your photos in the .wpp project file, select the **Embed Images** check box. (If you do not select this option your photos will remain 'linked' to the file.)

Now let's add some captions to our photos.

### To add a caption to a photo:

**1.**  With the first photo still selected, click the **Caption** column.

**2.**  In the **Caption** box type a caption for the selected photo.

| ☐ Image ▲ | Position | Caption |
|---|---|---|
| ☑ | 1 | European Long-Eared Eagle Owl |

3. Repeat steps 1 and 2 to add captions to the remaining photos.

   - or -

   To add the same caption to multiple photos, select their check boxes and type the caption into the box at the bottom of the **Caption** column.

When you are happy with the photos in the gallery, their order and their captions, click **Next**.

## Applying gallery styles and settings

Each gallery type offers a variety of professionally-designed preset template styles for you to choose from and modify to suit your needs.

### To apply gallery styles and settings:

1. Click through the templates displayed in the **Gallery Style** pane.

As you do so:

- The **Preview** pane shows how your photos will appear with the selected gallery style applied.

- The settings pane updates to display the various options you can adjust for the selected gallery style.

2. Select the gallery style you prefer and then adjust the settings as required. When you are happy with your photo gallery style and settings, click **Finish**.

Don't forget to save your work!

## Previewing your photo gallery

Now your photo gallery is created and added to your page, let's see what it looks like!

### To preview your photo gallery:

1. On the Standard toolbar, click the arrow to expand the **Preview site** drop-down list.

2. Select **Preview Page in {your web browser of choice}**.

## Editing your photo gallery and adjusting photos

Once you've inserted your photo gallery, it's easy to resize and move it on the page.

### To resize and move a photo gallery:

• To resize the photo gallery, select it with the ⬆ Pointer Tool and drag from a corner or line end handle. To constrain the photo gallery when resizing, hold down the **Shift** key when dragging.

Javascript galleries cannot be resized using the above method. The size of the JavaScript gallery must be set in the final window of the **Photo Gallery** dialog.

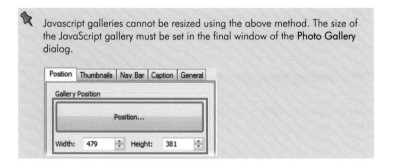

• To move the position of the photo gallery on your page, select it with the ⬆ Pointer Tool and drag.

Once you've placed the gallery on the page and previewed it, you may wish to make some changes. You can easily add, delete and organize photos, switch to a different gallery style, and adjust settings whenever you need.

**To edit a photo gallery:**

1. Right-click the photo gallery and click **Edit Photo Gallery...**

   - or -

   Double-click the photo gallery using the ▶ **Pointer Tool**.

2. The **Photo Gallery** dialog opens for editing and fine-tuning. To add hyperlinks to photos see below.


## Adding hyperlinks

Although a photo gallery can simply be used to display your photos, it can also act as a navigation tool to point visitors towards more information about the contents of the photo. This is achieved by adding a hyperlink.

In our example, each photo links to a new website page with more information about the bird of prey pictured.


**To add hyperlinks to photos:**

1. In the **Photo Gallery** dialog, click 🐾 **Edit Hyperlink.**

2. In the **Edit Hyperlinks** dialog, from the **Hyperlink Type** drop-down list, select **Use a different link...**

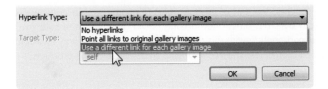

3. Click **OK**.

4. Select the photo check box and then double-click the **Hyperlink** column.

   - or -

   To add the same hyperlink to multiple photos, select their check boxes and then double-click the hyperlink box at the bottom of the **Hyperlink** column.

5. In the **Edit Hyperlink** dialog, select **Site Page** category, then select a site page from the **Page name** drop-down list.

6. Click **OK**.

We've reached the end of this tutorial. With some simple steps, we've created a stylish, professional-looking photo gallery. We're sure you'll enjoy experimenting with this powerful feature—a great way to display treasured memories, showcase artistic shots, or sell your products!

 See the tutorial, *E-Commerce*, on p. 177 for more information on using your website and images to sell products.

# Panels I: Designing with Panels

15 min

Panels have special properties which allow background elements to be stretched to fit the panel size. This makes designing a consistent look and feel for your site a really easy job! In this tutorial, we'll look at the use of panels as design elements.

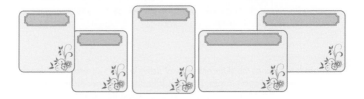

By the end of this tutorial you will be able to:

- Create a panel.

- Create a panel background.

- Create a stretching design.

- Create a fixed design.

- Insert a previously created design.

## Let's begin...

• In the Startup Wizard, in the Create section, click **Start New Site**.

• For the purpose of this tutorial, click **Cancel**.

This accepts the default settings and creates a new, single page site.

 We recommend that you complete the steps in the **Configure a New Site** dialog if you are starting a real site from scratch as it allows you to set up your site quickly and easily.

 In order to look at the different ways of using panels, we are not going to work to any particular design scheme. Instead, we'll work through a series of examples that should give you the tools you need in order to apply panels to your own site.

## Creating panels as design elements

When designing a website, you always want to aim for a consistent look and feel. This can be seen in the example below.

If you are quite adventurous with your design, you may find that it's a slow process trying to get everything to look the same. This is where the special properties of panels can help.

In this first example, we'll create a panel similar to the Popular Tags panel illustrated above. All design editing for panels is done in the dedicated environment of the **Design Studio**.

### To begin a new panel design:

1. On the **Quick Build** tab, in the **Layout Items** category, drag the **Panel** layout item to the page.

2. In the dialog, next to the background drop-down menu, click 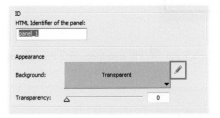.

The Design Studio opens to a blank (transparent) panel.

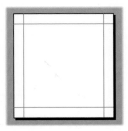

The next step is to start the design.

**To create a panel background:**

1.  On the Standard Objects toolbar, on the 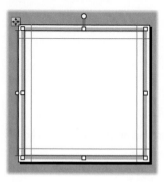 QuickShapes flyout, click the Quick Rectangle.

2.  Starting in the top left corner, drag on the page to draw a shape that covers most of the transparent panel. Ensure that the edges of the QuickShape are placed in between the grid lines.

3.  On the **Swatches** tab, click the Fill and then click the **Scheme 2** swatch.

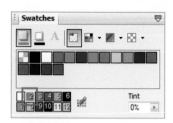

The fill updates.

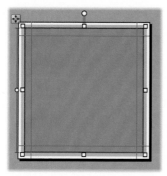

**4.** Drag the node control downwards to round the corners of the QuickShape.

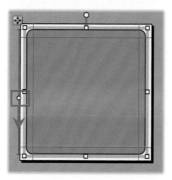

**5.** Before we finish, let's change the colour scheme. On the **Swatches** tab, click to open the **Scheme Designer**.

6. Select the **Melancholy** scheme, then click **OK** to exit. Our schemed object is updated to the new colours.

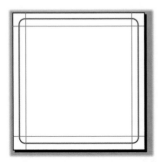

7. On the Standard toolbar, click **Commit Changes** to exit the **Design Studio**.

8. In the **Panel Properties** dialog, click **OK** to accept the default settings and exit.

9. The panel is placed on the page at its default size.

10. (Optional) Click and drag on the panel resize handles to set the size and shape of the panel.

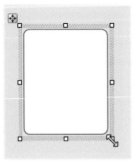

**Save now!** Click **File > Save As...** and choose a new name for your file.

## Special design properties

Take a moment to resize the panel by dragging on one of the resize handles. Notice that the corners always remain the same shape. This is because they were placed within the grid lines when we drew the object. We can use the special properties of the gridlines to create more advanced designs.

Let's do this now.

### To create a stretching panel design:

1.  Click the panel, then on the Panel context toolbar, click 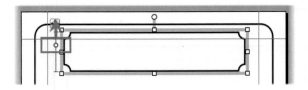 **Edit Panel**.

2.  In the dialog, next to the background drop-down menu, click ✏ to open the **Design Studio**.

3.  On the Standard Objects toolbar, on the ▭ˇ QuickShapes flyout, click the ▭ **Quick Rectangle**.

4.  Drag on the page to create a long, thin rectangle inside the existing background shape. This will make the surrounding box for our heading text. Drag the node control up to create the cut out corner effect.

Don't worry that the shape doesn't fit within the guides at this time as we can change this when we've completed the design.

5. With the shape selected, on the **Align** tab, ensure that **Relative to: Page** is selected and then click ⬒ **Centre Horizontally**.

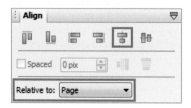

6. On the **Line** tab, in the drop-down list, change the line type to a double line.

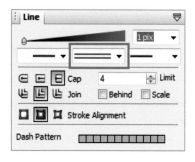

7. On the **Swatches** tab, click ⬚ **Fill** and then click the **Scheme 7** swatch. Next, click ⬚ **Line** and then click the **Scheme 8** swatch. The shape is updated.

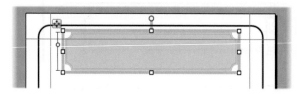

Now we need to change the guides so that the shape is enclosed. (We clicked on the workspace first to deselect the shape to make it easier to see the next steps.)

**8.** Drag the horizontal guide down so that the entire shape is contained within the new guide area.

This will prevent the shape from changing height when we resize the panel. However, we also want the two ends of the shape to stay the same if we change the width of the panel.

**9.** Drag each vertical guide inwards so that the left and right edges of the shape are contained within the vertical guides as illustrated.

This will 'fix' the corners in place, but will still allow the centre of the design to stretch or contract as necessary.

**10.** On the Standard toolbar, click ✅ **Commit Changes** to exit the Design Studio.

**11.** In the **Panel Properties** dialog, click **OK** to accept the default settings and exit.

On the page, you'll see that the panel design has been updated to reflect our changes. If you resize the panel, you'll see that the header design changes to fit the width of the panel, but never changes in depth.

Don't forget to save your work!

Finally, we'll place a small design in the bottom corner of our panel.

### To place a fixed design object on a panel:

1.  Click the panel, then on the Panel context toolbar, click ⬚ **Edit Panel**.

2.  In the dialog, next to the background drop-down menu, click ✎ to open the **Design Studio**.

3.  On the Standard Objects toolbar, on the ⬚ᵥ QuickShapes flyout, click the ❀ **Quick Petal**.

4.  Drag on the page to create a shape approximately 35 pix by 35 pix and position it as illustrated.

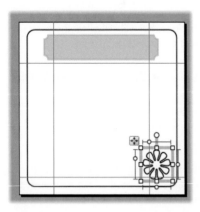

Notice that the shape does not quite fit within the grid lines. If we leave it like this and accepted our design, we'd start to get some strange behaviour if we changed the shape of our panel.

So what can we do to change this? We can't update the guides in the same way as before as this would affect our heading design. Instead, we need to fix the shape.

**5.** In the **Design Studio**, ensure that the QuickShape is selected.

**6.** On the Design Studio toolbar, in the 🔳▾ Horizontal scale flyout, click 🔳 **Right**.

**7.** On the Design Studio toolbar, in the 🔳▾ Vertical scale flyout, click 🔳 **Bottom**.

**8.** On the Standard toolbar, click ✅ **Commit Changes** to exit the Design Studio.

**9.** In the **Panel Properties** dialog, click **OK** to accept the default settings and exit.

On the page, you'll see that the panel design has been updated to reflect our changes. If you resize the panel, you'll see that the header design changes to fit the width of the panel, but the QuickShape always stays the same size and in the same place.

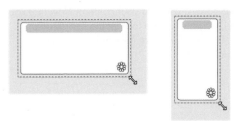

## To insert a previously created design:

1.  On the **Quick Build** tab, in the **Layout Items** category, drag the **Panel** layout item to the page.

2.  With the ⌐ cursor, click and drag on the page to pre-define the panel size. On release, the **Panel Properties** dialog opens.

3.  In the dialog, click the down-pointing arrow to view the **Background** flyout.

4.  In the **Site** category, select the design that we created earlier.

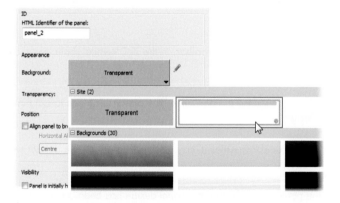

5.  Click **OK** to accept the default settings. (We'll look at all of the options in the next tutorial, *Panels II: Assigning Actions*, on p. 131.)

Once you have created your panels, you add your content! Now that you know how to design a panel, why not have a look at the next tutorial, *Panels II: Assigning Actions*. In this tutorial, we look at how to create floating panels and add actions.

# Panels II: Assigning Actions

 20 min

In the previous tutorial, we looked at panels as design elements. Panels have special properties which mean that they can have actions assigned to them. They can be made to hide until an item is clicked or hovered over, they can be free-floating, they can even be set to remain in view even when the window is scrolled! It makes the panel a really useful tool. In this tutorial we'll look at a few of the useful functions.

By the end of this tutorial you will be able to:

• Attach a floating panel to a browser window.

• Add objects to a panel.

• Add visibility actions.

• Hide and position a panel.

## Let's begin...

- In the Startup Wizard, in the Create section, click **Start New Site**.

- For the purpose of this tutorial, click **Cancel**.

  This accepts the default settings and creates a new, single page site.

 We recommend that you complete the steps in the **Configure a New Site** dialog if you are starting a real site from scratch as it allows you to set up your site quickly and easily.

 In order to look at the different ways of using panels, we are not going to work to any particular design scheme. Instead, we'll work through a series of examples that should give you the tools you need in order to apply panels to your own site.

## Floating panels

One use for a panel is as a 'floating' object that is permanently attached to the browser window, meaning that they do not scroll with the page. One of the primary uses for this is to have a navigation bar that is always accessible, either at the side of the top of the window.

By default, a panel added to a page scrolls with the page.

### To add a panel to a page:

1. On the **Quick Build** tab, in the **Layout Items** category, click the **Panel** layout item.

2. Starting at the top left of the page, with the cursor, click and drag on the page to create a panel approximately 90 pix high and spans the width of the page.

(Use the Hintline to help you to do this.)

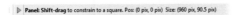

> **Panel: Shift-drag** to constrain to a square. Pos: (0 pix, 0 pix)  Size: (960 pix, 90.5 pix)

On release, the **Panel Properties** dialog opens.

3. In the dialog, click the arrow to view the **Background** flyout and in the **Backgrounds** category, select the first design. Click **OK** to accept the default settings and exit.

The panel on the page is updated.

To make it easy to see what's going on when we make our changes to our panel, we'll add a placeholder frame to our page.

## To add a placeholder frame:

1.  On the **Quick Build** tab, in the **Layout Items** category, click the **Text Frame** layout item.

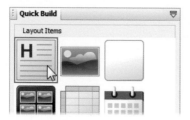

2.  With the  cursor, click and drag on the page to insert a frame that fills the remaining blank space on the page.

3.  On the **Text** menu, click **Insert** > **Fill with Placeholder Text**.

### Previewing the (default scrolling) panel:

1. On the Standard toolbar, click the arrow to expand the 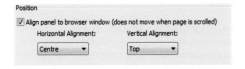 **Preview site** drop-down list.

2. Click the **Preview in Window (Internet Explorer)** option.

3. Drag the scroll bar up and down. Notice that the panel also scrolls out of view. We can change this in the panel properties.

4. Click **Close Preview** to return to the open document.

### To attach panel to a browser window:

1. Click to select the panel, then on the Panel context toolbar, click **Edit Panel**.

2. In the **Panel Properties** dialog, select the **Align panel to browser window**.

Position

☑ Align panel to browser window (does not move when page is scrolled)

Horizontal Alignment:     Vertical Alignment:

Centre ▼          Top ▼

3. The default alignment options are **Centre** and **Top**. These are ideal for our needs so click **OK** to accept the changes.

4. Preview the page again and drag the scroll bar up and down. Notice that the panel no longer scrolls. However, the text scrolls over the top of the panel which isn't ideal. To stop this, we need to change the z-order of the panel.

5. Click **Close Preview** to return to the open document.

## To bring the panel to the top of the z-order:

• Select the panel and on the Arrange toolbar, click  **Bring to Front.**

Preview the page again and drag the scroll bar up and down. The text now scrolls neatly behind the panel.

 To complete the panel, all you need to do is add a navigation bar! A panel behaves like a container, so when an object is added on top of a panel, it inherits the panel properties. Try it out for yourself!

 Panels and master pages

It's common practice to place navigation elements on a master page so that it's easy to achieve consistency throughout your website. However, if you do this and still want your navigation panel to be permanently on view on top of your content, then you need to remember to adjust the order of the master page in the **Objects** tab. To do this, display the **Objects** tab and then drag the master page containing your panel and navigation bar (Master A in this example) to the top of the stack.

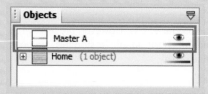

All objects placed on the master page will now display on top of your content. You will need to do this for each page that uses the master page. For more information on using master pages, see WebPlus Help.

Don't forget to save your work!

## Hidden panels

Panels can also be hidden until some action is performed, normally either a click or a hover-over. This means that they can be used to display extra information while keeping your visitor on a specific page. They can also be used for surveys and advertisements. It's also possible to have a panel on view when a visitor enters your site and then provide a button for them to close (hide) the panel.

 When creating hidden panels, it's always best to design your panel before you hide it!

 For clarity, we created the next panel on a new, clean page.

### To create a basic panel:

1.  On the **Quick Build** tab, in the **Layout Items** category, click the **Panel** layout item.

2.  Starting at the top left of the page, with the cursor, click and drag on the page to create a large rectangular panel.

    The **Panel Properties** dialog opens on release.

3.  In the **Backgrounds** category, select a basic design (we chose plain white) and click **OK** to accept the default settings and exit.

To make our panel useful, we'll need to add some elements. Panels can contain virtually anything—images, text, QuickShapes, buttons, galleries, smart objects, advertisements... You'll need to think carefully about what you're trying to do by using a panel. For now we'll just add an image and a gallery object.

### To add objects to a panel:

1.  On the **Quick Build** tab, in the **Layout Items** category, hold the **Ctrl** key and click the **Picture** layout item.

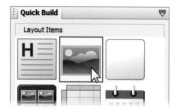

2.  With the ⁺▣ cursor, click and drag inside the panel to place your empty frame.

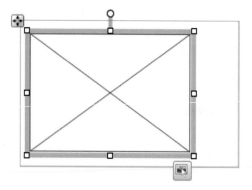

**3.** Add an image to the frame. (We used an image from the **Tutorials** asset pack. See the tutorial, *Pictures,* on p. 65 for detailed information.)

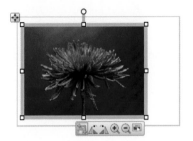

**4.** Next, on the **Assets** tab, click ⬜ **Browse...** to open the **Asset Browser**.

**5.** In the **Categories** section, click the **Graphics** category and then in the Search box, type "Tutorials". The tutorials graphics are displayed in the main pane.

**6.** Click the **Add All** ⊘ button. The green ⊘ shows that the assets have been added to the **Assets** tab. Click **Close** to exit the **Assets Browser**.

**7.** Drag the red cross from the **Assets** tab to the top right corner of the panel.

Our panel is now complete. If you preview it in a browser, you'll see that it doesn't really do anything exciting. Let's apply an action to the close button that we added.

### To add an action to an object:

1. Right-click on the cross object that we added to the panel and in the menu, click **Actions...**

2. In the dialog, on the **Actions** tab, click **Add...** and from the drop-down list, click **Visibility**.

3. In the **Show/Hide Panel Action** dialog:

- Select the panel to apply the action to from the **Panel ID** drop-down list. (We only have a single panel in this example.)

- In the **Event** drop-down list, select **Hide on Click**.

- (Optional) To increase or decrease the fade speed, adjust the slider.

- Click **OK**.

4. The assigned actions are displayed in the dialog.

**5.** Click **OK** to return to the page.

**6.** Preview your panel in a browser.

If you click on the cross, the panel should disappear. You'll notice that we now have no way of reopening our panel. Although this is actually useful behaviour for advertising panels, we need to add another object to show the panel. (If you still have your preview open, close it now.)

**7.** On the **Assets** tab, in the **Graphics** category, drag the purple instant photo icon to the **page**. (Ensure that it doesn't touch or overlap the panel.) Resize it so it's about double its original size.

We're now going to add a visibility action to the new object.

**8.** Right-click on the new object and in the menu, click **Actions...** (If this is unavailable, you might be trying to apply an action to a group. See the note on p. 142 for a solution.)

**9.** In the dialog, on the **Actions** tab, click **Add...** and from the drop-down list, click **Visibility**.

**10.** In the **Show/Hide Panel Action** dialog:

* Select the panel to apply the action to from the **Panel ID** drop-down list. (We only have a single panel in this example.)

* In the **Event** drop-down list, select **Show on Click**.

- (Optional) To increase or decrease the fade speed, adjust the slider.

- Click **OK**.

**11.** The assigned actions are displayed in the dialog.

If you preview your panel again, you'll see that clicking on the cross closes the panel, and clicking on the photo icon opens it again. Well done, you've created a panel with actions!

 **Why is the 'Actions' option greyed out?**
If you try to add an action to a grouped object, you'll find that the option is disabled. However, all is not lost! All you need to do is to convert the group into a picture first and then you can add the actions. To do this right-click the grouped object and then click **Convert to > Picture...** Next, select the picture format and if necessary, adjust the quality settings. When you click **OK**, the grouped object is converted to a picture with the specified format.

Now that we've created our panel and tested our design, we can hide the panel when the page first opens. If you still have your preview open, close it now.

**To hide and position a panel:**

1.  Click the panel, then on the Panel context toolbar, click  **Edit Panel** to open the **Panel Properties** dialog.

2.  Select the **Panel is initially hidden** option and click **OK**.

    The page updates to show a hidden panel object (green question mark icon) instead of the panel.

3.  Drag the hidden panel object into position next to the photo icon. This sets the position of the top-left corner of the panel when it opens.

4.  Finally, with the hidden panel object still selected, on the Arrange toolbar, click  **Bring to Front**.

    This ensures that the panel opens on top of the photo icon.

**5.**   Preview the panel to test out its new functionality!

 Don't forget to save your work!

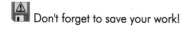 You can also quick hide or show the panel by selecting the panel and then clicking ⊞ **Hide Panel** on the Panel context toolbar.

That's all there is to it. You should now have everything you need to create various panels in your own website. Good luck and have fun! Don't forget to have a look at the tutorial, *Panels I: Designing with Panels,* on p. 119 for information on designing with panels.

# Panels III: Sliders

 15 min

If you want to really add some style to your website, then you might want to consider using sliders. Sliders allow you to create a wide variety of subtle animated elements on your website, from banners and advertisements to photo galleries and even for navigation!

By the end of this tutorial you will be able to:

* Identify and select an existing slider on a page.

* View alternative slider panels.

* Modify slider content.

* Modify slider animation.

* Add a slider to your page.

## Let's begin...

1.  On the **File** menu, click **Startup Wizard...**

2.  In the Create section, click **Use Design Template.**

3.  In the dialog:

    •   In the **Theme Layouts** list on the left, click **Doodle.**

    •   Click **Open.**

        The Home page opens in the workspace.

## What are sliders?

Sliders are essentially a type of animated panel. They get their name from the most commonly used animation effect which uses a slide transition effect from one slider panel to the next. Sliders are often used to simply display different images in a similar way to a photo gallery, but they can also be used to create elements such as animated banners, great looking navigation elements, and news items. In fact, sliders can even be programmed to display certain panels on a specific date, meaning that they can make a great tool for creating advertisements or for highlighting a special event.

The theme layout that we've opened has two pages that contain sliders, the Home page and the Products page. We'll look at the slider on the Home page first.

## To preview your site in a Web browser:

1. Click the arrow to expand the 🖥▾ **Preview site** drop-down list.

2. Select **Preview Site in** {your web browser of choice}.

3. Your site will open in a new browser window.

   On the Home page, you'll see that the slider alternates a set of three images by scrolling them from right to left.

4. For now, close the browser window and return to WebPlus.

## Identifying and selecting sliders

Sliders come in many forms and all of the ones available in WebPlus can be customized to suit your needs. The slider on the Home page is one of the more simple types. We'll start by customizing this and then have a look at some of the other sliders available.

If a slider contains pictures, and is placed on the page with other pictures, it can be hard to tell at first glance where the sliders are. The easiest way to identify and then select your sliders is by using the **Objects** tab.

### To identify and select an existing slider:

1.  On the **Objects** tab, click the small + to expand the Home page objects.

2.  In the **Show** drop-down list, select **Slider**.

3.  All sliders on the page are displayed. Click on the slider object to select it.

On the page, you can see that the slider panel has been selected.
Note the slider controls at the bottom of the slider.

Also notice the slider context toolbar at the top of the workspace.

## To view alternative panels on a slider:

1. With the panel selected, click once on the  Show Next Panel
   button. A second panel is displayed.

**2.**  Repeat the process twice more. Notice that after the next picture, there is a blank panel.

This is a foreground panel. Anything placed on this panel will appear on top of all of the other panels as they're displayed.

**3.**  On the **Objects** tab, select **Slider foreground** from the **Show** drop-down list. Each of the different slider panels is listed in the tab.

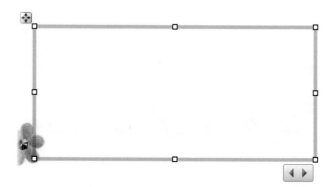

Clicking on any of the entries in the tab will select that panel on the slider.

Using filters in the Objects tab.

To make it easier to identify and select different items on you page, the **Objects** tab has several filters for you to use. When dealing with sliders, the following two filters are probably the most useful:

**Show: Slider** is useful to help you to identify all of the sliders on your page. Clicking on the slider entry in the Objects tab selects the main slider panel

**Show: Slider foreground** is useful to identify the individual panels that are used within a specific slider.

## Modifying slider content

Sliders can contain virtually any type of content that could be placed on the page. The professionally designed sliders included with WebPlus primarily contain pictures, shapes or text. The pictures are placed within a frame which means that they can easily be replaced with your own content. Let's do this now.

(For more information on working with pictures and frames, see the tutorial, *Pictures*, on p. 65.)

First of all, we'll import the tutorial pictures into the **Assets** tab. However, you can use your own images if you want to.

### To add Picture assets to the Assets tab:

1.  On the **Assets** tab, click ⊡ **Browse...** to open the **Asset Browser**.

2.  In the **Categories** section, click to select the **Pictures** category. The pictures from all installed packs are displayed in the main pane.

3. In the main pane the assets are categorized by the Pack file that they belong to. In the **Tutorials** pack, click **Add All** ⊘.

   The green ⊘ shows that the assets have been added to the tab.

4. Click **Close** to exit.

Now that we've imported our picture assets, we can add them to the frames on the slider.

### To change a picture on a slider panel:

1. On the **Objects** tab, click on the first slider panel entry to select the first slider panel.

2. Click once on the picture. Note how the picture frame controls are now displayed instead of the slider controls. This is because the picture is now selected and not the slider.

3. Drag the picture of the beach umbrella from the **Assets** tab onto the slider. The current picture will be highlighted to show that it will be replaced.

4. On release, the picture is replaced. Adjust as necessary using the picture frame controls.

5. Next we'll repeat the process to replace the next picture. First, we need to select the slider panel either by pressing **Ctrl + R** or by clicking **Select Parent** form the **Edit** menu. This selects the parent (container) object such as the slider panel. (**Ctrl + R** also works when dealing with standard panels and forms.)

   When the panel is selected, the slider panel context toolbar is displayed at the top of the workspace.

6. With the panel selected, click once on the ▶ **Show Next Panel** button.
   (If the next panel is the blank foreground panel, click the ▶ **Show Next Panel** button again.)

**7.**   Repeat steps 2 - 4 to change the picture to that of the beach house.

**8.**   Once again, press **Ctrl + R** to select the slider panel and click once on the ▶ **Show Next Panel** button. Repeat steps 2 - 4 to change the picture to that of the surfer.

Now would be a good time to preview the page to see the changes in action.

**9.**   Click the arrow to expand the 🖥▾ **Preview site** drop-down list and select **Preview Page in** {your web browser of choice}.

Once you've finished, close the browser.

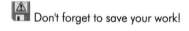 Don't forget to save your work!

Next, we'll edit the foreground panel and see how this effects our slider. This time, we'll select our foreground panel by using the slider context toolbar.

## To edit the foreground panel:

1. Using the **Objects** tab, select the slider.

2. On the slider context toolbar, in the Panel Selector drop-down list, click **Foreground**.

The foreground panel is displayed. Now we can add our content directly to it.

3. On the **Quick Build** tab, in the **Layout Items** category, click the **Text Frame** layout item.

4. With the 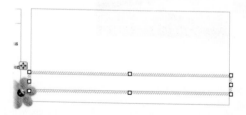 cursor, click and drag on the slider to insert the frame that spans the width of the slider.

5. On the **Swatches** tab, click **A** **Text** and then click the white swatch.

6.  Next, click on the text frame border. It will become a solid line when selected.

7.  On the **Swatches** tab, click  **Fill** and click the Scheme 11 Swatch.

8.  Click inside the text frame and on the text context toolbar, change the text size to 24pt and set the text to centre-align.

9.  Type "Beach Retreat".

Let's now see what happens when we preview our changes.

10. Click the arrow to expand the  **Preview site** drop-down list.

11. Select **Preview Page in {your web browser of choice}**. As you can see, the foreground items display on each slider.

The foreground panel is a great place to put information that you always want people to see. Examples of its use could be for contact information, a button or a watermark. As the foreground panel itself cannot be animated, you could add a picture to it. This way you can use a single image with animated text panels. You'll find examples of different kinds of sliders in the **Asset Browser**.

## Modifying slider animation

As well as amending slider content, it's also very easy to change the animation style. We'll look at this now.

### To edit slider animation type:

1.  Using the **Objects** tab, select the slider.

2.  On the slider context toolbar, click  **Edit Slider**.

    The **Slider** dialog opens. From here we can change the animation style, timing and whether or not it loops continuously.

3.  On the **Options** tab:

    *   In the **Animation style:** drop-down list, click **Opaque fade**.

    *   Change the **Panel display time (ms)** to **6000**.

    *   In the **Start panel** drop-down list, select **3 : Panel**.

    *   Click **OK** to exit the dialog.

4.  Click the arrow to expand the  **Preview site** drop-down list and select **Preview Page** in {your web browser of choice}.

You can see that the slider animation has now changed to a subtle fade, each panel displays for 6 seconds and that the slider begins with panel 3. Once you've finished, close the browser.

## Adding a slider to a page

If you want to add a new slider to your own site, you'll need to look no further than the **Assets Browser**. Here you'll find many different types of slider ready to be added to your page and customized to suit your requirements.

### To add sliders to the Assets tab:

1.  On the **Assets** tab, click 🗀 **Browse...** to open the **Asset Browser**.

2.  In the **Categories** section, click to select the **Sliders/Panels** category. The sliders 🖵 and panels 🖻 from all installed packs are displayed in the main pane.

3.  In the **Pack Files** section, hold the **Ctrl** key while clicking on the **Tutorials** pack. Only the sliders installed with the tutorials are now displayed in the main pane.

4.  In the **Tutorials** pack, click the **Add All** ⊘ button.

The green ⊘ shows that the asset has been added to the tab.

**5.** Click **Close** to exit the dialog and return to the page.

The sliders are displayed in the **Assets** tab.

Next we'll add one of these sliders to a new page.

### To create a new blank page:

**1.** On the **Site** tab, click the arrow on the ⊞ ▾ **Add new page or link** drop-down list and select **New Blank Page...**

**2.** In the **Page Properties** dialog, type in a page name, title, and file name—we chose to create a 'Sliders' page—and then click **OK**.

The new page is displayed in the workspace ready for us to add our sliders.

### To add a slider to the page:

**1.** On the **Assets** tab, the **Sliders/Panels** category should be displayed (if not, click the header).

**2.** Drag the spaceships slider onto the page.

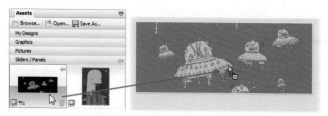

**3.** You can now view and edit the slider.

## Slider examples

Now that you can identify and edit a basic slider, let's look at two more slider examples.

### Example 1

First we'll preview the site and look at the slider we have just added to the new page. As you can see, this slider autoplays but also has a slider navigation bar beneath the slider. Clicking on any one of the 'dots' takes you to the relevant panel.

If you add additional panels to the slider, the navigation bar will automatically update to include them.

You can edit the appearance of slider navigation bars in much the same way as standard navigation bars (although there are fewer options). Select the navigation object and then click **Edit Navigation Bar** on the context toolbar.

For more information, see WebPlus Help.

## Example 2

Preview the site and look at the sliders on the Products page. If you hover over any of the sliders on the Products page, a coloured information panel is displayed which also contains a small, magnifying glass button.

If you place the mouse pointer over the button and click, a separate window known as a lightbox appears containing the product information.

In WebPlus, if you select and edit one of the product sliders, you'll see that it comprises of two panels using an overlay effect. The first panel contains an image (e.g., the product image) and the second panel contains the information. The button on this panel is hyperlinked to the relevant product information page which is set to appear as a lightbox.

 We've looked at sliders which contain mainly images. However, you'll find more fully customizable sliders of all styles in the **Sliders** asset pack located within the **Asset Browser**. We recommend that you spend some time familiarising yourself with these sliders as you're bound to find one that's suitable for your needs.

As you can see, sliders are extremely useful objects. When added to your page, they not only make the page look good, but they can also add a lot of functionality. Have fun!

# Contact Forms

 15 min

Web-based forms are useful tools. In this tutorial, we're going to add a contact form to a 'Contact Us' page that we created on our fictional SCUBA diving club site to allow site visitors to contact the webmaster and submit their personal comments.

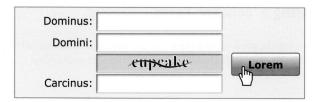

By the end of this tutorial you will be able to:

- Create a web-based email contact form.

- Edit form objects.

- Display a form page in a lightbox object.

 Go to **http://go.serif.com/resources/WPX6** to download the following tutorial project file(s):

portfolio_basic.wpp

---

 This tutorial assumes that you have already registered for a **Serif Web Resources** account as you will need to log in to access the Smart objects. If you are unsure how to do this, see the online tutorial *Serif Web Resources* or see WebPlus Help.

## Let's begin...

**1.** On the Standard toolbar, click  **Open**.

**2.** Navigate to the **portfolio_basic.wpp** file, select it and click **Open**.

The 'Home' page is displayed in the workspace.

## Creating a 'contact' form

It's important to show visitors there is a live person or business behind your website—this adds credibility and legitimacy to your online presence.

By providing easy ways for visitors to communicate with you, you will establish this credibility. You may wish to add your postal address, telephone numbers and email address to your website, though this carries with it the risk of unwanted spam.

Instead we recommend providing visitors with a secure contact form for them to contact you directly.

> Forms can be used to collect a variety of data from site visitors. Data collected can be as simple as the person's name and email address, or a whole host of personal information. How much data you ask for on a form really depends on what you need it for.

Let's get started.

## To create a contact form using the Form Wizard:

1.  Open the **Contact** page in the workspace by double-clicking it on the **Site** tab.

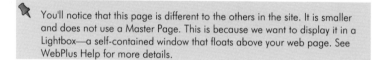

You'll notice that this page is different to the others in the site. It is smaller and does not use a Master Page. This is because we want to display it in a Lightbox—a self-contained window that floats above your web page. See WebPlus Help for more details.

2.  On the **Quick Build** tab, in the **Forms** category, click the **Form** item.

3.  To insert the form at default size, position the  cursor where you want the form to appear and then click once.

    The **Form Wizard** dialog opens.

4.  In the dialog, click **Use and adapt a standard form** and then click **Next**.

**5.** Click any list item to display a preview of the selected form in the **Preview** pane.

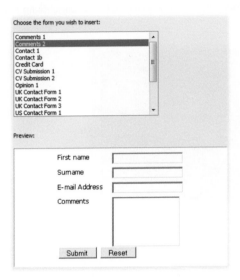

Select the **Comments 2** form and click **Next**.

**6.** The next dialog screen allows you to customize the form layout and add additional items. The default layout is almost right, but we need to add a CAPTCHA object. Click the **CAPTCHA** button.

**7.** In the **Add New Control** dialog, type "Are you human? Type the letters you see." in the **Enter label** box and click **OK**.

The new object is displayed at the bottom of the list.

8.  Next, with the CAPTCHA object select, click  **Move Up** twice to move the object above the Submit Button.

9.  Click **Next**.

---

### Form controls

The building blocks of a form comprise a mixture of text, graphics, and **form controls**. Form controls collect visitor data and can be added, moved, and modified in a similar way to other WebPlus objects.

Form control fields include buttons, text boxes, check boxes, radio buttons, combo boxes, and so on. A typical form is made up of a combination of these fields.

The CAPTCHA object is linked to your Serif Web Resources account and is an anti-spamming control. It helps to prevent junk email from non-human web traffic. The site visitor must type the graphical word into the input field. If they match, the visitor is allowed to continue.

**10.** In the next dialog:

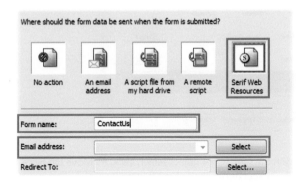

- Select **Serif Web Resources**.

- Type a name for your form. (This must not contain spaces or special characters.)

- Next to the email address field, click **Select**.

**11.** In the **Form Email Targets** dialog, select the email address linked to your **Serif Web Resources** account. Click **Edit**.

**12.** Type a subject for your form dialog and then type a confirmation message that the user will see when they submit the form.

When you're ready, click **Update**.

**13.** Your change will be displayed be displayed in the **Available Email Targets** section.

Click **OK** to exit.

 If you want to add a new email target address, you'll need to add this in the **New Target** section. You'll also need to confirm the email address via the confirmation email before you can receive form submissions to it.

**14.** Finally, click **Finish**.

The form is inserted on the page.

Don't forget to save your work!

## Editing form layout

You'll notice that some of the objects don't fit on the page and that the objects themselves don't look that great:

• The form field labels are too dark and don't stand out.

• The CAPTCHA object label is too long.

• The form **Submit** and **Reset** buttons don't line up with the other input fields.

• There is no title!

Luckily, WebPlus lets you move and edit form controls just as you would any other object. We'll demonstrate this now...

### To move and edit form buttons and labels:

**1.** Select the CAPTCHA object label and drag the corner handle to resize it.

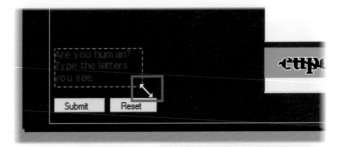

2. Drag a selection marquee over the input fields to select them all and then drag them into place next to the text.

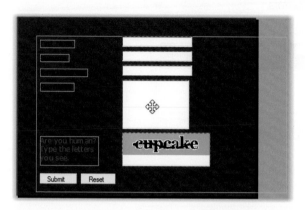

3. Next, drag a selection marquee around all of the text labels.

 Form labels are simply HTML text frames. This means that you can edit them in exactly the same way as an HTML frame that you place on the page.

**4.** On the **Swatches** tab, click the Scheme 2 swatch.

**5.** On the **Align** tab ensure that **Relative to: Selection** is displayed, and click the **Right** align button.

The text objects are aligned.

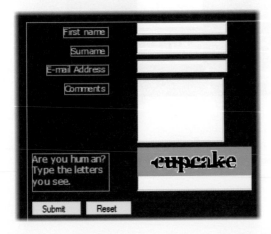

**6.** Next, select both the **Submit** and the **Reset** button and drag them into place below the CAPTCHA object.

**7.** Finally, click the form object to select it and then resize it to fit on the page by dragging on the resize handle.

We also added an HTML text frame to the top of our form to create a title. The text was set to Heading 2.

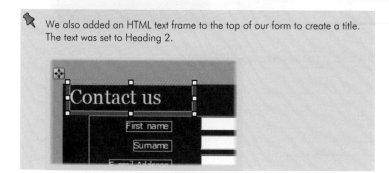

 Don't forget to save your work!

8. On the Standard toolbar, click the arrow to expand the 💻▾ **Preview site** drop-down list.

9. Select **Preview Page in** {**your web browser of choice**} to see what your form will look like.

## Displaying a form in a lightbox

• Double-click on the 'Home' page on the **Site** tab.

If you look carefully at the **Site** tab, you'll notice that the Contact page is not included in the navigation. Instead, we're going to link to it from the 'contact us' text at the top of the Master page.

### To link a form page to a lightbox:

1. On the Home page, click the 'contact us' text object and then click ⁺ᴬ **Edit on Master Page**.

2. Select all of the 'contact us' text and on the Web Properties toolbar, click 🔗 **Hyperlink**.

3.  In the **Hyperlinks** dialog, on the Hyperlinks tab, in the left category
    list, click **Site Page**. Next in the **Page Name** drop-down list select
    **Contact**.

4.  Click to display the **Target Window** tab, and in the **Target Window**
    **or Frame** section, select **Lightbox** from the drop-down list.

    We'll accept the default **Width** and **Height** for the lightbox and click
    **OK** to accept the settings.

5.  On the Standard toolbar, click the arrow to expand the 🖥 **Preview**
    **site** drop-down list and select **Preview Site in** {your web browser of
    choice}.

6.  Finally, click on the link to test it! Your form should display neatly in
    its own lightbox.

That's it! Once your form is published, visitors to your site can type their
details directly into the text boxes provided. When they click **Submit**, the
information is sent via **Serif Web Resources** to the email address you
specified when you created the form.

# E-commerce

 25 min

If you've ever bought anything online, you'll know how simple the process can be as a buyer. But how difficult is it to set up your own e-store? Fortunately with WebPlus, the process is simple. Over the next few pages, we'll show you how by creating a page to sell photographic prints.

By the end of this tutorial you will be able to:

* Choose and configure your e-commerce cart provider.

* Creating an e-commerce form.

* Use an existing e-commerce form as a template for your other objects.

 Go to **http://go.serif.com/resources/WPX6** to download the following tutorial project file(s):

📥portfolio_basic.wpp

## Let's begin...

1.  On the Standard toolbar, click  **Open**.

2.  Navigate to the **portfolio_basic.wpp** file, select it and click **Open**.

    The 'Home' page is displayed in the workspace.

    **Save now!** Click **File > Save As...** and choose a new name for your file.

In the following sections, we'll configure a shopping cart provider, and insert and configure an e-commerce form.

## Choosing a Shopping Cart Provider

Any website that supports e-commerce activity will typically use a shopping cart and payment gateway. There are many third-party shopping cart providers that can be used. Each provider offers the same basic features and with WebPlus, it's easy to set up your e-commerce site using one of our selected providers, all of which offer a good range of features.

In this project, we've chosen PayPal© as the provider most suited to sell some photo prints. We'll now step you through the signup and configuration process.

Our example uses PayPal© as our shopping cart provider. Some cart providers offer additional features and depending on your needs, these may or may not be important to you. Use the provider's Help pages to find out more about unique shopping cart features.

## To setup and configure a PayPal shopping cart:

1. On the **Site** tab, double-click the **Shop** page entry to display the page.

2. On the **Quick Build** tab, in the **E-commerce** category, drag the **E-commerce** item to the page.

3. In the **E-commerce Configuration** dialog, select the **PayPal** option and choose one of the following options:

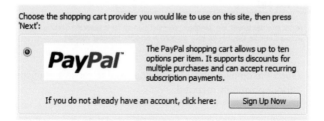

- If you already have a PayPal account, click **Next**.

- If you don't have an account, click **Sign Up Now**. The PayPal site opens in your browser. Follow the instructions provided to register and set up an account. When you have finished, return to WebPlus.

**4.** In the **PayPal Configuration** dialog:

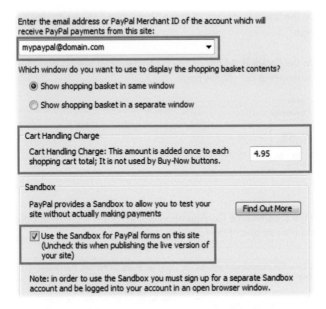

- Type the email address where you want to receive notification about payments received.

- Set the **Cart Handling Charge**, i.e. your default overall shipping charge.

- (Optional) If you want to use PayPal's **Sandbox**, a test tool for trying out your shopping cart before going live, select this option.

  To use the Sandbox, you must set up a separate test account (in addition to your live PayPal login) through PayPal's Developer Central site. Click **Find Out More** to do this.

- Click **Next**.

**5.** Click **Use the PayPal Minicart**. For now, leave the default settings (you can always change them later) and click **Finish**.

Once you have finished setting up your account, the PayPal object dialog will immediately open to allow you to create the PayPal e-commerce form.

 You can change your e-commerce settings at any time by going to **Tools > E-Commerce Configuration**.

 When you create subsequent forms, WebPlus will remember your e-commerce settings and open the e-commerce form dialog as soon as you drag the e-commerce object to the page.

## Creating an e-commerce form

WebPlus makes it really easy to add e-commerce objects, either as a form or link, depending on the characteristics of the item(s) you are selling. In our example, we'll add a form since it offers more flexibility and allows for some user interactivity.

 For information on the differences between forms and links and why you might choose one over the other, see WebPlus Help.

 Our site uses **picture frames** to display the images. This makes it very easy to create thumbnails of our e-commerce objects and means that we can replace images very easily while retaining aspect ratio. See the tutorial, *Pictures*, on p. 65 for more information on using frames.

### To insert a PayPal form:

1.  (This step is only applicable once a shopping cart provider has been configured.)

    On the **Quick Build** tab, in the **E-commerce** category, drag the **E-commerce** item to the page.

2.  In the **Add PayPal Object** dialog:

    *   Select the email address that is to receive the payment information.

    *   WebPlus assumes that the email address set during shopping cart configuration is used. If you want to use a different address—for example, the address you specified when you set up your Sandbox, clear the **Use the site default address** box and select a different address to override the site default.

    *   Select the **Add to Shopping Cart Form** option.

    *   Click **Next**.

**3.** In the **Button Image** dialog:

- Select the **Use a standard image** option.

- Select the image of your choice.

- Click **Next**.

**4.** In the **Item Details** dialog, enter the following information:

- **Item Name:** The name of the item for sale. Try to make this descriptive as it will appear as the item description on the invoice produced by the cart. We typed 'Artist's print: City'—the title of the photograph displayed in the first picture frame.

- **Item ID:** If you have a specific product code reference, enter it here. We left ours blank.

- **Currency:** Choose the currency required from the drop-down list.

- **Price:** Type the price of the item.

- Click **Next**.

5.  The **Item Description** can be used to add extra details about the sale item.

    - As we have three different sizes of print for sale, list the price of each size in the description.

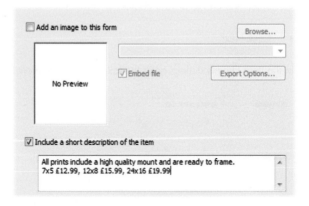

    - We already have an image, so we don't need to add another. Click **Next**.

6.  In the **Item Options** dialog, click **Add Multiple Option...**

**7.** In the **Multiple Option** dialog:

- In the **Name** box, type 'Size'.

- In the **Prompt** box, type 'Size:'.

- Select **Option changes price**.

- Select the **Combo Box** option.

- Click **Add Option...**

For information on the other options in the dialog, see WebPlus Help.

**8.** In the **Option** dialog:

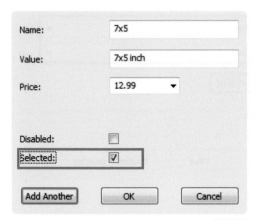

| Name: | 7x5 |
| Value: | 7x5 inch |
| Price: | 12.99 ▼ |
| Disabled: | ☐ |
| Selected: | ☑ |

[Add Another]  [OK]  [Cancel]

- In the **Name** box, type '7x5'.

- In the **Value** box, type '7x5 inch'.

- In the **Price** drop-down list, select 12.99.

- Click the **Selected** check box—this sets the item as the default option when the page opens.

- Click **Add Another**.

**9.** Repeat step 8 to create a '12x8' option, but this time:

- In the **Price** field, type '15.99'.

- Do not select the **Selected** check box—you can only set one default!

- Click **Add Another**.

**10.** Repeat step 9 to create a '24x16' option at '19.99' and then click OK.

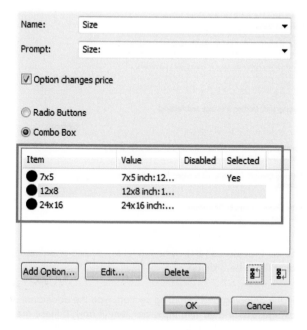

Your **Multiple Options** dialog should now list the three options you specified. Click **OK**.

**11.** The **Item Options** dialog displays again, allowing you to add further options. We don't want to do this so click **Next**.

**12.** In the **Item Details** dialog:

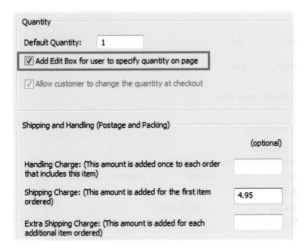

- Select the **Add Edit Box** option to let the customer define the quantity to be ordered.

- In the **Shipping and Handling** section, type the additional charges associated with the order item (if any). If these are left blank, the default profile set in PayPal will be used.

- Click **Next**.

**13.** In the **Extra Customer Information** dialog, ensure **Customer prompted for address** is displayed in the drop-down list and click **Next**.

**14.** In the **Payment Pages** dialog, leave the default settings and click **Next**.

**15.** In the **Form Layout** dialog, because we have more than one pricing option, clear the **Show price on form** option and click **Finish**.

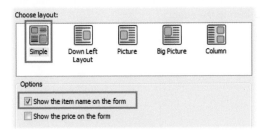

**16.** The new form is inserted on the page. If it isn't in the correct place, click to select the form object and drag it into position beneath the first title.

**17.** If necessary, you can move and adjust the individual form objects, and edit their appearance, as you would any other WebPlus object. We adjusted the position and size of the form and some of the objects.

Don't forget to save your work!

We're now going to insert another e-commerce object into the space created—a **View Cart** button.

**To insert a View Cart button:**

1. On the **Quick Build** tab, in the **E-commerce** category, drag the **E-commerce** item to the page.

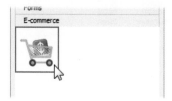

2. In the **Add PayPal Object** dialog:

   • Select the email address you used previously.

   • Select the **View Shopping Cart Link** option.

   • Click **Next**.

3. In the **Button Image** dialog:

   • Select the **Use a standard image** option.

   • Select the image you want to use.

   • Click **Finish**.

4.  The button is inserted at default size. If necessary, drag it into position on your form.

5.  Preview your page in your web browser. Check that you can:

    *   Select a **Size** from the drop-down list.

    *   Edit the product **Quantity**.

    *   Add items to your shopping cart.

    *   View your shopping cart.

Don't forget to save your work!

## Using an existing form as a template

If you're happy with the way your first product looks and functions, you can use it as a template for your other objects by simply copying and editing the form.

We'll do this next...

## To copy and edit the form:

1. Click inside the form object to select it.

2. Hold the **Ctrl** key and drag down to create a copy of the objects. Position these next to the second image.

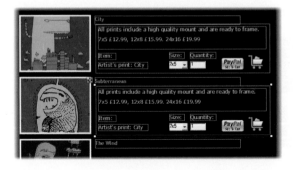

⚠ In our sample store, we only need to change the name of each item as all other options (for example, print size and price) stay the same.

It is important that you do this by editing the form and not by editing the text boxes directly as it's the form information that gets passed to the invoice.

When you create your own e-commerce site, the extent of the changes required in these dialogs will depend on the type of items you are listing for sale. If your items are very different, you may prefer to simply create each form from scratch, rather than copying and editing your first page as we have done here.

3. Right-click on an empty part of the form and select **Edit e-commerce Form...**

4. In the **Add PayPal Object** dialog, click **Next**.

5. In the **Button Image** dialog, click **Next**.

6. In the **Items Details** dialog, check the details displayed and replace any that do not apply to your new item.

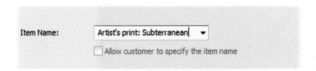

(In our case, we only needed to type in the new name for the image 'Subterranean'.)

Click **Next**.

7. In the **Item Description** dialog, replace any of the options that have changed for this new item. If the same options apply, as in our case, simply click **Next** to proceed.

8. Unless you need to make changes, click **Next** until you come to the **Form Layout** dialog. Ensure that the **Reformat form now** option is cleared and click **Finish**.

   The form is updated with the new details, but we can't see the update as the frame is too small.

**9.** Drag the right resize handle until the text fits inside the frame.

**10.** Preview the page in your browser.

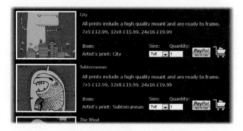

Now that you have two objects in place, it's easy to add the rest of your product list. Your finished page should look something like ours.

Congratulations, you've created your first e-commerce website! We hope you've enjoyed the exercise and wish you every success in your e-commerce ventures.

# Previewing & Publishing

 25 min

Once you have made your site, the next step is to publish it to the internet. We'll take you through the steps in this tutorial.

By the end of this tutorial you will be able to:

- Preview your site in WebPlus at different screen resolutions.

- Preview your site in different Web browsers.

- Prepare your website for publication.

- Publish your website.

- Maintain your published website.

 Go to **http://go.serif.com/resources/WPX6** to download the following tutorial project file(s):

portfolio.wpp

## Let's begin...

1. On the Standard toolbar, click  **Open**.

2. Navigate to the **portfolio.wpp** file, select it and click **Open**.

   The 'Home' page is displayed in the workspace.

> We are going to use the 'Illustration portfolio' project in this tutorial. However, if you have already created your own website, you can use it to undertake the steps outlined below.

## Previewing your website

With the vast number of web browsers available, it's important to test your site to ensure that it will be viewed in the way that you intended. Before you upload your site to the masses, we'll show you how to test your site in different browsers.

### To preview your site in WebPlus:

1. On the Standard toolbar, click the arrow to expand the 🖥▾ **Preview site** drop-down list.

2. Click the **Preview in Window (Internet Explorer)** option.

   (If you have created a large site, there may be a slight delay while the site is exported to display in a web browser.)

Once exported, WebPlus displays the site preview in a built-in Microsoft Internet Explorer window.

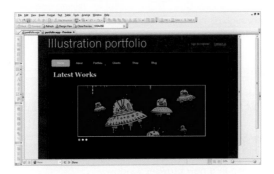

**3.** To switch between your regular design view and the **Preview**, simply click on the tabs at the top of the workspace area.

**4.** Even if your site navigation is incomplete, you can jump to different pages using the Page Selector at the bottom left of the workspace.

**5.** When you have finished, click 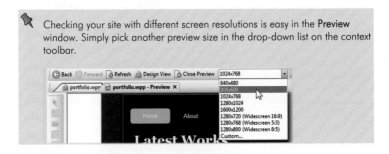 **Close Preview**.

Checking your site with different screen resolutions is easy in the **Preview** window. Simply pick another preview size in the drop-down list on the context toolbar.

If you make any changes to your design, your site will be 'republished' when you next switch to **Preview**. You can also preview your site, or single page, in an actual browser window. This is useful for testing compatibility with other browsers such as Firefox, Chrome, Safari or Opera. WebPlus automatically detects if alternate browsers are installed.

## To preview your site in a Web browser:

1.  Click the arrow to expand the  **Preview site** drop-down list.

2.  Select **Preview Site in {your web browser of choice}**.

3.  Your site will open in a new browser window.

 If you have installed a browser that does not appear in the Preview List, you may need to add it manually. For more information see *Previewing your website* in WebPlus Help.

Though exact statistics vary, the most popular browsers (in no particular order) are Firefox, Google Chrome and Internet Explorer. Each browser works differently so it's important to see how your site appears in each of them. Other browsers such as Opera (especially for mobile devices) and Safari are also supported by WebPlus. Browsers can be freely downloaded and it's worth installing a few different ones and testing your website in each of them.

## Preparing your website for publication

We'll assume that our design looks great in a range of browsers. Now it's time to publish our site to a live location. Even though you may have saved your website as a WebPlus project, it's not truly a 'website' until you've converted it to files that can be viewed in a Web browser. WebPlus does this automatically when you publish the site.

---

 Useful terms to know:

• **FTP** - File Transfer Protocol—this is the standard way of uploading your website's files from your computer to your web host.

• **URL** - Universal Resource Locator—this is the 'address' where your site resides on the web.

• **Web Host** - this is a company which provides web space for you to store the files necessary to display your website pages on the internet.

---

### Publishing options

WebPlus can publish your site in several ways:

• **Publish to a Disk Folder** - lets you use your site as a network-based Intranet, write it to CD-ROM for distribution, or upload it manually to an internet server using FTP software.

• **Publish to the Web** - publish your page or site directly to a Web server so that it can be viewed over the internet.

• **Quick Publish to Web** - publish only the page that you are currently working on directly to the Web server.

---

 **Note:** The next steps assume that you have dedicated space on a web server. If you are unsure how to access this, contact your Web host. See the online tutorial, *Managing Your Web Presence*, for more information on web hosting.

## To prepare your website for web publication:

1. Check your page names, file names, and picture export settings in the **Edit > Site Properties...** and **Tools > Image Export Manager...** dialogs. (For details, see WebPlus Help.)

2. In 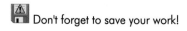 **Site Manager** (on the Default context toolbar), use **Site Checker** to check your site for problems such as non-Websafe fonts, invalid anchors and hyperlinks, and so on. (For details, see WebPlus Help.)

When you are satisfied all issues with your website have been resolved, you can set up your FTP account and publish to the world wide web.

> You will only have to set up your FTP account the first time you publish your site to the web.

 Don't forget to save your work!

## To set up your FTP account:

1. On the Standard toolbar, click the arrow to expand the 🔽 **Publish site** drop-down list.

2. Click 🔽 **Publish to Web**.

3. In the **Publish To Web: Get Hosting** dialog, click **Add Details**.

4. In the **Site Base URL** dialog, type in the URL for your website in the text box, e.g. http://www.illustrationportfolio.com.

   The **Account Details** dialog will open.

5. When publishing to the Web you'll need to provide the following information, most of which you can obtain from your Web host. (When you receive this information, usually displayed on-screen or sent by email on purchase of your web space, it is worth printing out for your own records and for later reference.)

Details

| | |
|---|---|
| Account name: | Illustration portfolio |
| FTP address: | illustrationportfolio.com |
| Port number: | 21 (Default FTP port 21, unless in implied mode) |
| Folder: | (May be case-sensitive) |
| Username: | illustrationportfolio |
| Password: | ●●●●●●●●● ☑ Save password |
| Passive mode: | ☑ (Uncheck this if you have problems connecting) |
| Web site URL: | http://www.illustrationpor (optional) |

- **Account name:** A descriptive name for this connection. This can be any name of your choice. You'll use it to identify this account in WebPlus (you may have more than one).

- **FTP address:** The URL that locates the internet-based server that will store your files—it will look similar to a Web address but often starts 'ftp://'. The FTP address is supplied by your Web host.

- **Port number:** Unless directed by your Web host, leave the **Port number** set at 21. This is the default port used by most FTP servers for file transfer.

- **Folder:** Allows you to upload sites to sub-folders of your main website's address. You can leave this blank unless you are directed otherwise by your Web host, or you want to publish to a specific subfolder of your root directory. (This may also be needed to correctly route your upload specifically to your own Web space.)

- **Username:** Specified by your Web host—this is often case-sensitive.

- **Password:** Specified by your Web host—this is often case-sensitive.

- **Passive Mode:** Leave checked (by default) unless you experience upload problems.

- **Website URL:** The web address of your site—it often starts 'http://' or 'https://'.

  For more information about setting up your account details, see *Publishing to the web* in WebPlus Help

**6.** When you've entered all your information, click **OK**.

Before you proceed further, it's a good idea to test your account settings to ensure there are no issues with connecting to the internet.

### To test your account details and connection:

- In the **Upload to server** dialog, click **Test**.

  WebPlus will attempt to connect to your hosting account.

  You will be informed if the connection has been successful:

  - If unsuccessful, select your FTP Account from the drop-down list and click **Edit** to review your settings.

  - If successful, click **Update Account**—your new FTP account and settings are displayed in the **Publish to Web** dialog.

Once you've set up your FTP account and can connect your computer to the host, publishing to the Web is simply a matter of transferring files.

## Publishing to the web

With your FTP account set up and project ready-to-go, let's get onto the exciting task of getting your site onto the web!

 If you're currently in the main workspace, click **File** > **Publish Site** > **Publish to Web...** to access the **Publish to Web** dialog.

### To publish your site to the web:

1. In the **Publish to Web** dialog, your current FTP account details should be displayed. If not, select an FTP account from the drop-down list.

2. In the **Page Range** tree, select which page(s) to publish. To publish the entire site, select the **Publish All Pages** option.

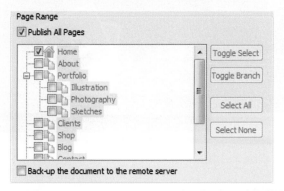

3. Click **OK**.

   WebPlus will convert your design into HTML pages with associated graphics and other files, then begin to upload your site to the internet, showing individual file progress and overall progress.

4.  When WebPlus has exported the selected pages, close the **Uploading files** dialog—the **Web Site Publishing** dialog opens.

5.  To view your site online, choose your browser from the drop-down list and click **View this URL**.

Your browser will launch showing the specified URL.

## Maintaining your website

The great thing about websites is the ability to update them frequently at no extra costs—in fact, visitors will expect your website to be up-to-date with all the latest information. With WebPlus, it's quick to update a modified website which has been previously published.

**To update a previously published website:**

1.  With the **portfolio.wpp** project still open in your workspace, use the Page Selector at the bottom left of the workspace to select the **Photography** page.

2.  Select the grouped objects on the page and then press **Delete**.

3.  On the **Quick Build** tab, in the **Layout Items** category, drag the **Photo Gallery** layout item to the page.

4.  Work through the dialog to place a photo gallery onto the page.

    See the tutorial, *Photo Galleries*, on p. 107 for more information.

Don't forget to save your work!

5.  Click **Publish Site > Publish to Web...** from the **File** menu.

6.  In the **Publish To Web** dialog:

    -   Select an FTP account from the drop-down list.

    -   In the **Page Range** section, ensure only the **Photography** page is selected.

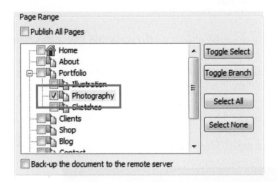

    -   Click **OK**.

7.  In the Uploading Files dialog, select **Incremental Update** or **Full Upload**.

    -   **Incremental Update:** If you choose this option, WebPlus will export your site and compare the exported files to those already on the server. It will only upload files that are new or have changed since the last upload. This option can also check for missing files. Incremental updates are great when you want to quickly replace minor elements of your site!

    -   **Full Upload:** If you choose this option, WebPlus will upload all the files, regardless of whether they have changed since the last upload.

        In both cases you can instruct WebPlus to delete uploaded files that are no longer required by selecting this option in the dialog.

By only uploading pages which have changed (and selecting **Incremental Update**) you will notice that the web upload is much quicker. You can view your updated page in a browser.

If your web server cannot accommodate spaces in file names, complete the following steps to have WebPlus remove the spaces and symbols from file names when they are published:

## To convert file names:

1.  On the **Edit** menu, click **Site Properties...**

2.  Click the **File Naming** category and then select the **Remove spaces** and **Remove symbol character** options.

3.  Web pages are normally published with lower case file names. Select **Make lower case** to get WebPlus to do this for you.

4.  If you've already published your site, you'll need to republish to fix the problem. This also improves site reliability.

 You can maintain your published website further by using the **Maintain Website** dialog (accessible from **File** > **Publish Site**). For more information, see *Maintaining your website* in WebPlus Help.

That's it! You've published your site to the Web for all to see! As you can see, WebPlus makes it very easy to publish your site and upload new content.

 If you're having problems we suggest you check your provider's website to find the information you need, or contact their customer support team.

**Note:** Serif cannot supply you with this information unless you have a **Serif web hosting account**.

# Search Engine Optimization

This tutorial will help you develop good techniques which should help improve your website's visibility on search engines.

By the end of this tutorial you will be able to:

- Use page names, titles, and file names to improve searches.

- Use keywords and descriptions effectively.

- Understand how good website content can improve results.

- Generate search engine files.

- Submit your site to search engines.

## What is Search Engine Optimization?

A search engine is a tool that a person searching on the internet can use to find information. Search Engine Optimization (or SEO) is a process of configuring a web site and performing some other online tasks in order to help increase a site's popularity in internet search results, without paying for advertising slots. The higher a website appears naturally in a list of search engine results, the more relevant or popular it will seem in the eyes of people searching, so website setup and relevant search terms should be worth some of your time and thought.

SEO is not necessary for every website and there are other internet marketing strategies that can be more effective in generating traffic to your site. What most people actually require is to make their website search engine friendly. Your website doesn't have to appear in search engine rankings for people to access it once a site is live; if your visitors already know your website's web address (URL) they can access it directly using the address bar at the top of their internet browser. SEO is particularly helpful in acquiring new website visitors that are interest-matched to your products, services, the information on your site, and sometimes your location.

This tutorial will help you try and improve your website's visibility in search engine results, using proven techniques as recommended by search engine operators.

## Let's begin...

1.   In the Startup Wizard, in the Create section, click **Start New Site**.

2.   In the **Configure a New Site** dialog, type the name of your site in the **Site Name** input box.

     This is important to search engine listings—we'll discuss this in more detail later.

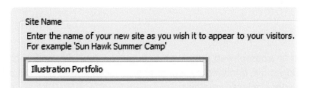

> **Site Name**
>
> Enter the name of your new site as you wish it to appear to your visitors. For example 'Sun Hawk Summer Camp'
>
> | Illustration Portfolio |

3.   Then proceed through the dialog using **Next** and, when finished, click **Finish**.

 Here are some simple rules to consider when creating a site name:

*   Use title case capitalization and use "&" not "and".

*   Do not use descriptive information or marketing hype about the site.

*   Do not add a string of keywords.

*   Do not use an acronym only—provide the name in its entirety and then the acronym in brackets.

*   Do not use the site's web address (URL) or include the words 'Welcome to', 'Website', or 'Web Page'—unless these are part of the site name as shown on the website.

## Making your site search engine friendly

To help get you noticed, there are recommended strategies that you can use to make your website search engine friendly.

 We cannot tell you how to get your site ranked high in search engine results. Search engine companies carefully guard their algorithms on creating results to prevent people 'cheating' their way up the listings.

### Linking

Hyperlinks to external web pages, other pages on your site, and anchors on long pages are analyzed by search engine technologies and will add weight to your content's credibility.

 If you work frequently with specific businesses and clients, or have family and friends with websites, why not link to their websites and ask them to link to yours—network via the net!

See the tutorial, *Creating Hyperlinks & Anchors*, for more information on adding hyperlinks and anchors to your own website.

### HTML tags

HTML text frames offer you the ability to design with HTML-compliant styles. This means that you can format text using heading styles from H1 to H6. H*n* styles are given priority over ordinary body text styles (the default) in internet search engines, with the H1 tag being given highest priority.

See the tutorial, *Frame Text*, for more information on applying text styles.

## ALT and TITLE tags

It's possible to add some HTML text tags (**ALT** and **TITLE** tags) to your pictures and other objects that will be published as images. Using pertinent keywords for these text strings adds further weight to your site's content.

See the tutorial, *Pictures*, for more information on assigning ALT and TITLE tags.

# Page names, titles and file names

In WebPlus, there are three ways of identifying each page: **name**, **title**, and **file name**. Each of these works differently to help search engines list your website pages:

- **Name**: is not directly used by search engines, but becomes the default page title, if a title is not provided.

- **Title**: is stored both in the published HTML code (for use by search engines) and in the visible title bar of viewers' Web browsers.

- **File name**: is used by search engines to distinguish pages.

## To modify page name, title, and file name:

1. On the **Site** tab, click the arrow on the  **Add new page or link** drop-down list and select **New Blank Page...**

2. In the **Page Properties** dialog, on the **Navigation** category:

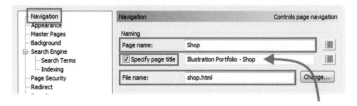

- In the **Page name** text box, type the name of your page.

- Select **Specify page title** and then update the title of your page—use the same rules as described for site names.

   The **Site Name** you specified in the **Configure a New Site** dialog (at the beginning of this tutorial) is automatically added to each page title!

- In the **File name** text box, type a descriptive file name for your page (it must be lower case and cannot contain spaces).

3. Click **OK**.

   With your page name, title, and file name set, your website it now easier for search engines to identify—plus visitors to your website will see the page title in their browser.

You can update the page name, title, and file name of existing pages by right-clicking the page in the **Site** tab and selecting **Page Properties...**

Strong page names, titles, and file names work particularly well alongside site and page keywords and descriptions. Together they provide a wealth of information to help search engines identify and categorize your website—as well as strengthening your site's credentials.

## Keywords and site description

When choosing **keywords**, think about your site and its content. Do a little research to help you find out what keywords people would search with to find your site, as well as thinking about what you offer in particular. Also note variations of UK and US English words.

It's important that your keywords appear in the site content as well, otherwise this can be seen as keyword stuffing—a less reputable SEO technique that can actually result in your site being ranked lower than it otherwise would be.

Having carefully chosen a set of keywords, let's integrate them into your site.

### To set keywords for a site:

1.  On the **Edit** menu, choose **Site Properties...** and then click the **Search Engine** > **Search Terms** category.

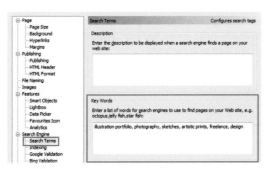

2.   Enter your choice of keywords in the lower text box. Separate your keywords and keyword phrases with commas.

Click **OK** when you're done.

The site-wide keywords you enter will be included on each page of your site.

 Here are some simple rules to consider when creating keywords:

- Keep them focused.

- Ensure they represent your site and page content accurately.

- All your site keywords **must** appear somewhere in your site text content.

- Do not stuff your website full of keywords. This can be extremely detrimental to search engine rankings.

If you have a multi-page site and certain pages offer unique content, you can supplement the keyword and description information on a page-by-page basis. Remember, any keywords you add per page must appear somewhere in your page's text content.

### To set keywords for a page:

1.   On the **Site** tab, right-click the 'Home' page and click **Page Properties...**

2.   Click the **Search Engine > Search Terms** category and enter your choice of keywords in the lower text box. Separate your keywords and keyword phrases with commas.

To include keywords and phrases from your Site Properties, ensure
**Include global keywords...** is selected.

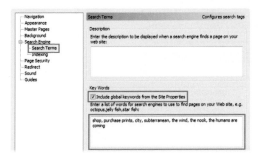

3.  Click **OK** when you're done.

    Having page-specific keywords and descriptions that better match
    the body text on each page will help improve your site's chances of a
    higher search engine ranking.

## Site and page description

The site and page descriptions are used by search engines to help
determine a rank for your site among search results—it also appears
below the hyperlinks in searches, giving users an idea of what displays on
the site and page. Aim to have a clear, concise description.

 Here are some simple rules to consider when creating descriptions:

  • Keep it clear, informative, and concise, and ensure it represents your site
  and page content accurately.

  • It should contain your chosen keywords and keyword phrases, but should
  not excessively repeat them.

  • Use correct spelling, punctuation, and sentence structure, while also
  avoiding acronyms.

  • Use "and" not "&", unless the sentence normally appears with "&" on your
  site.

You can enter your site and page descriptions in the **Search Terms** category in the **Site Properties** and **Page Properties** dialogs.

 You may wish to write your site/page description first, and then pick out keywords within the description.

### To preview your page in a Web browser:

1. Click the arrow to expand the 🖥️▾ **Preview site** drop-down list.

2. Select **Preview Page** in {your web browser of choice}.

3. In your browser, choose to view '**Source**' (usually available from the browser's **View** menu).

```
<meta name="keywords" content="shop, purchase prints, city, subterranean, the
wind, the nook, the humans are coming, illustration portfolio, photography,
sketches, artistic prints, freelance, design">
<meta name="description" content="The Illustration Portfolio shop offers you
the opportunity to purchase prints at a range of sizes. The latest prints on
sale are City, Subterranean, The Wind, The Nook, and The Humans Are Coming.">
```

As you can see from our coloured HTML snippet, the keywords and description are stored in a meta tag—a named piece of information within the HTML code.

 Keywords and other search engine related tweaks can also be accessed via the **Site Manager**. For more information about either the Site Manager or assigning keywords to your site, see WebPlus Help.

Let's now consider what happens once your site is finished and published—how will search engines find it?

Some search engine companies use automated systems (often called **spiders**) to find and help rank sites. These electronic arachnids follow links to your site from known resources (or find your site in the search engine's own directory) and analyze your site's keywords as well as other content.

Many search engines, including Google™, do not use meta tag keywords in their search engine technology, so you'll need to go beyond the WebPlus Site and Page Properties dialogs. Let's explore this further…

## Text content

The **text content** of each page is crucial. Writing engaging content is the first step for improving search results! Make sure your chosen site keywords are well represented throughout your site and page keywords appear within the text on your page. Including keywords in the first paragraph of a page is of particular importance.

In addition to writing finer detail in your content, you should also include broader descriptions and terms frequently. You may also like to ensure important words in your text appear in **bold** or *italic* formatting, and give them prominence in page's first text paragraph. These attributes may lead to those words being given more prominence in search rankings.

It's not difficult to write content with the keywords in mind. Using your keywords in your main text can also make up for any key terms which are published as part of a graphic—search engine 'spiders' can't read text that has been converted to a picture.

 You may wish to write your site/page text content first, and then pick out important sections to create your site/page descriptions and keywords.

# Search engine file generation

Web crawlers discover pages from links within your website. Sitemap.xml supplements this data and allows crawlers to pick up all of the URLs. Essentially, sitemap.xml is a list of all of the pages that you really want indexing and provides extra information about each URL, such as how often the page changes, when it was last updated, how important it is compared to the other site pages, etc.

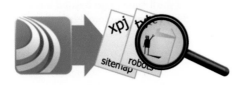

All of this information can really improve your site rankings—WebPlus takes care of writing the file for you.

## To create a sitemap.xml file:

1.  On the **Edit** menu, click **Site Properties...**

2.  In the **Site Properties** dialog, click the **Search Engine** > **Indexing** category, then:

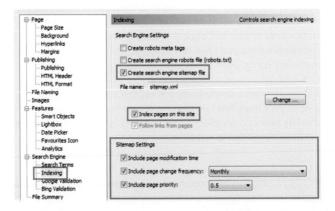

- Select the **Create search engine sitemap file** option.

  We recommended you do not change the file name.

- Select **Index pages on this site** and choose which **Sitemap Settings** you wish to apply.

  If you want to display page priority, it's worth remembering that 0.0 is the lowest and 1.0 is the highest setting.

- Click **OK**.

**3.** If the **Site Base URL** dialog appears, click **Cancel** for now.

Individual pages on the site can be given different settings to the rest of the site, or be entirely excluded from the sitemap file.

### To modify a sitemap.xml file for individual pages:

**1.** On the **Site** tab, right-click the 'Home' page and click **Page Properties...**

**2.** In the **Page Properties** dialog, click the **Search Engine > Indexing** category, then:

- Select the **Override site search engine settings** check box.

- Once you have finished making your changes, click **OK**.

Don't get confused between the search engine file **sitemap.xml** and the **Site map** navigation tool. Although they have similar names, sitemap.xml is a search engine tool only.

A navigation Site map is a collection of hyperlinks that acts like a dynamic table of contents. It is also highly useful in search engine optimization and we recommend adding a Site map to your website. See the tutorial, *Navigation Bars*, on p. 95 for more information.

Whereas sitemap.xml tells the Web crawler to index the page and follow its links, **robots.txt** does the opposite. Essentially, it provides a list of pages that should not be indexed. This can be useful if you do not want to include one or more links that go to external sites. Robots.txt generally works in conjunction with the robots meta tags for more precise settings. For more information, see WebPlus Help.

## To create a robots.txt file:

1. On the **Edit** menu, click **Site Properties...**

2. Click the **Search Engine > Indexing** category:

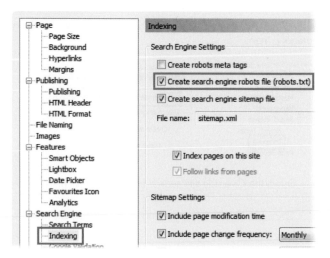

- Select the **Create search engine robots file (robots.txt)** check box.

- Click **OK**.

**3.** If the **Site Base URL** dialog appears, click **Cancel** for now.

For the overall site properties, it is best to leave the **Index pages on this site** option selected. If you have a page that you do not want to index, you can do this from the **Site Manager** dialog.

 A good page to remove from indexing would be a Search Results page.

### To exclude a page from index:

**1.** On the Default context toolbar, click  **Site Manager**.

**2.** In the **Site Manager** dialog, click the **Page Properties > Indexing** category, then:

- Ensure **Override Site** is checked for the page that you do not want to index.

- Uncheck **Index Page**.

**3.** Click **Close**.

In addition to all the preparation you've made directly to your website, some search engine companies accept submissions of sites for inclusion in their search results, sometimes at a price. This may be a handy strategy for improving traffic to your website if needed.

## Search engine submissions

You can submit your website (generally for free) to popular search engines (such as Google and Bing) to help get your website listed. The engines will then use "crawlers" to index your site. Detailed information about submitting your site to search engines can be found on the internet.

In addition, you should try to get your site listed in the free online directory called the **Open Directory Project**, www.dmoz.org.

We've only scratched the surface here on optimizing your website for inclusion in search engine listings—the internet has many other tips and tricks to help you along. Furthermore, search engine technology is constantly evolving and becoming ever more complex. The main thing to remember is that keeping your website up to date with engaging content is really the best way of optimizing your website. Best of luck!

The tips throughout this tutorial have focused on honest methods of improving rankings (known as 'White Hat SEO') rather than devious methods (known as 'Black Hat SEO') which can actually harm search engine rankings. Try searching on "Black Hat vs White Hat SEO" using your favourite search engine for more information and tips.

# Navigation Bars

WebPlus X6 has a selection of preset **Navigation Bars** for use in your sites. All preset navigation bars are schemed, and customizable in the **Button Studio**.

The following categories of presets are available:

- Block
- Graphic
- Highlight
- JavaScript

- Speech
- Standard
- Tab
- Traditional

## To add a preset navigation bar to your page:

1 Drag the **Navigation Bar** element from the **Quick Build** tab (Navigation Items category) to your page.

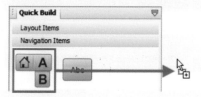

- or -

From the **Insert** menu, click **Navigation>Navigation Bar...**

The **Navigation Bar Settings** dialog opens.

2 From the dialog's **Type** tab, browse navigation bar categories in the left pane, expanding menu options if needed.

Browse the preset navigation bars in the right pane and then select your chosen navigation bar to preview the appearance of pop-up menus

3 Click **OK**.

The following pages provide previews of the preset **Navigation Bars** provided with **WebPlus X6**.

See *Inserting Navigation Bars* in WebPlus Help, or the tutorial, *Navigation Bars*, on p. 95 for more information on adding, creating and editing Navigation Bars.

## Block

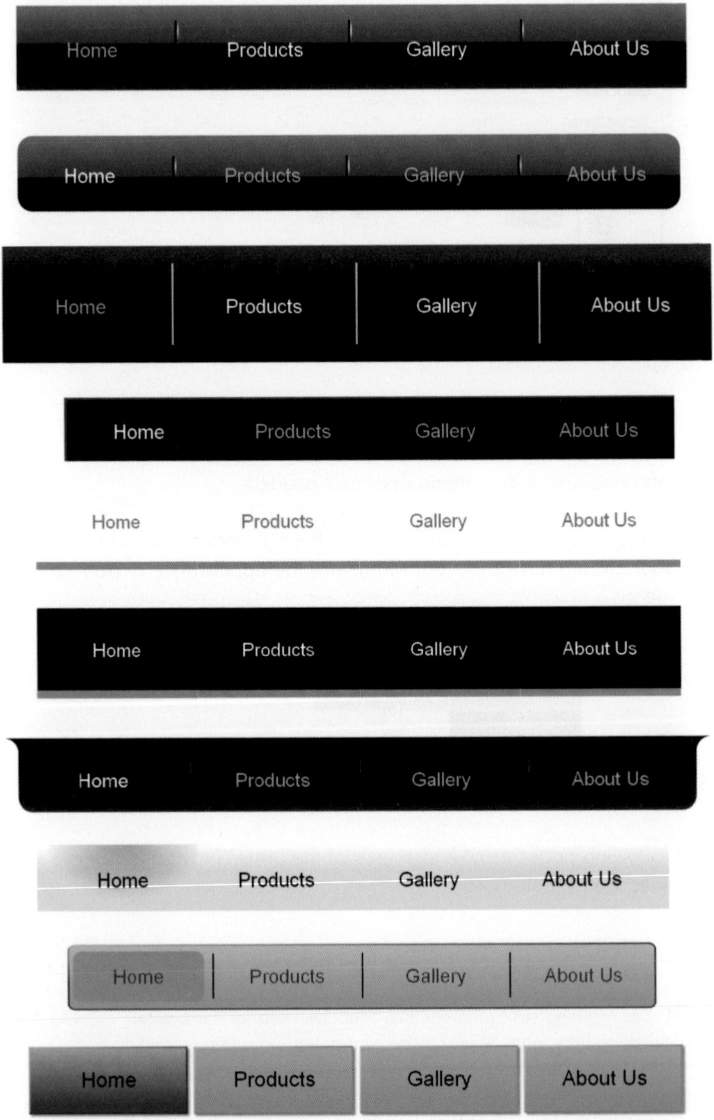

Home     Products     Gallery     About Us

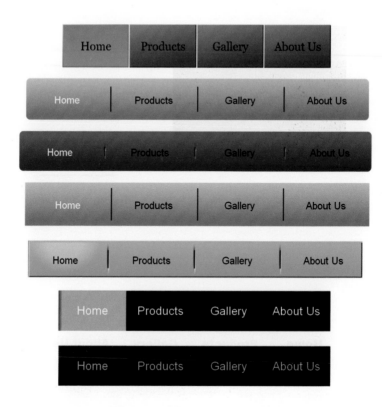

## Block > Vertical

## Graphic

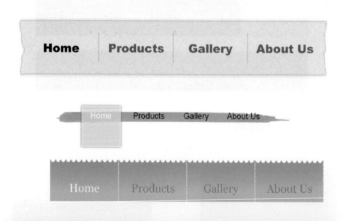

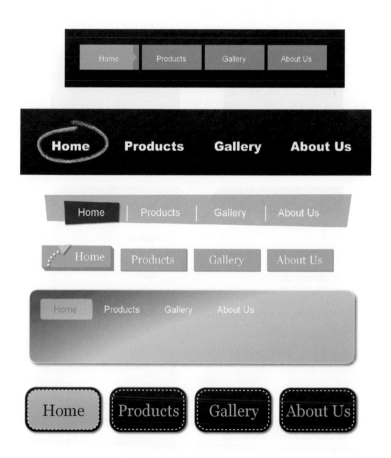

## Highlight

## JavaScript

Home Products Gallery About Us

**Home Products Gallery About Us**

Home Products Gallery About Us

Home Products Gallery About Us

[Home] [Products] [Gallery] [About Us]

Home | Products | Gallery | About Us

1 | 2 | 3 | 4

Home - Products - Gallery - About Us

Home * Products * Gallery * About Us

## JavaScript > Vertical

Home
Products
Gallery
About Us

Home
Products
Gallery
About Us

Home
Products
Gallery
About Us

Home
Products
Gallery
About Us

## JavaScript > **Combo**

Home ▾

Home ▾ | Go

## JavaScript > **Sitemap**

| | |
|---|---|
| Home | Home |
| Products | Products |
| New | New |
| Recommended | Recommended |
| Special Offers | Special Offers |
| Gallery | Gallery |
| About Us | About Us |

## JavaScript > **Folding**

| | |
|---|---|
| **Home** | |
| Products | ▶ |
| Gallery | |
| About Us | |

## Speech

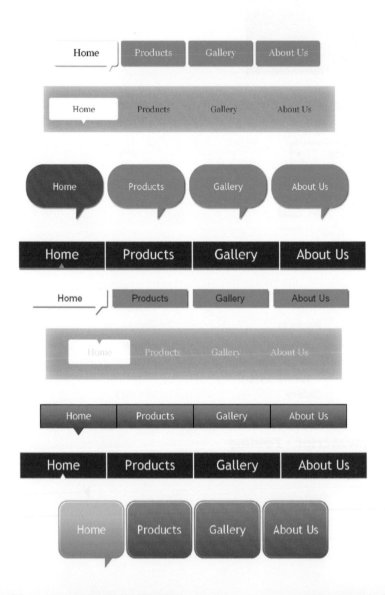

## Standard

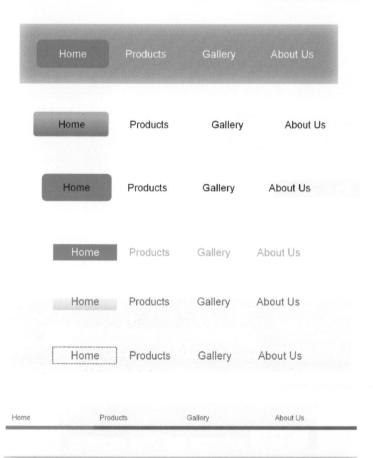

## Tab

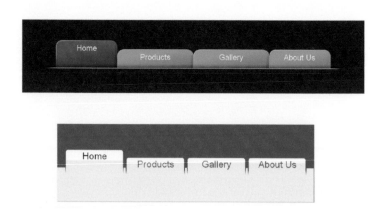

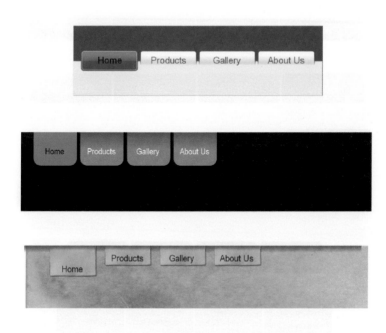

## Traditional

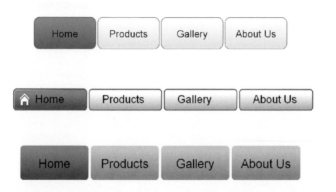

# Colour Schemes

In WebPlus, a colour scheme is a group of **12** complementary colours. Schemes in WebPlus work much like a paint-by-numbers system, where page elements in a layout are assigned specific colours by number.

If you use a pre-supplied theme layout, you can dramatically alter the appearance of your website just by swapping the colour scheme. See the tutorial, *New Site from Template*, on p. 7 and *Theme Layouts* on p. 255.

Colours are stored in specific swatches, numbered 1 to 12, hosted on the **Swatches** tab.

These swatches represent the site's colour scheme. From here, you can assign colours to page elements to make them schemed.

## **To apply a colour scheme:**

1  On the **Swatches** tab, click the  button (next to the colour swatches).

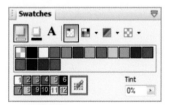

The **Colour Scheme Designer** opens. In the Scheme Manager pane, you'll see an assortment of named schemes.

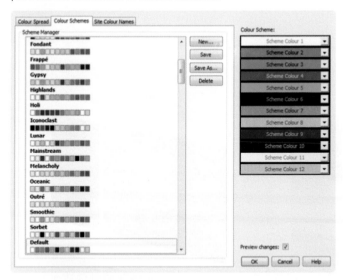

2  On the **Colour Schemes** tab, click a named scheme to apply the scheme to your website.

See *Using colour schemes* in WebPlus Help or the online tutorial, *Colour Schemes*, for more information.

# Colour Schemes

WebPlus offers an impressive selection of pre-designed **Colour Schemes**, which you can apply to your own site or use to update a **Pro Template** or **Theme Layout**.

The following pages provide previews of the pre-designed **Colour Schemes** provided with **WebPlus X6**.

**Ague**

**Comic**

**Coral**

**Default**

**Desert Rock**

**Dilettante**

**Eccentric**

## Fawn

**Fondant**

# Frappé

# Gypsy

# Highlands

**Holi**

**Iconoclast**

**Lunar**

## Mainstream

## Melancholy

**Oceanic**

**Outré**

## Smoothie

## Sorbet

# Theme Layouts

WebPlus provides a selection of both desktop and mobile Theme Layout templates that you can use as starting points for your own sites.

Accessible from the Startup Wizard, the Theme Layouts offer a range of layout styles. Each layout comes complete with picture and text placeholders, and offers a choice of purpose-built site pages.

Each theme includes the following pages:

For desktop:

- About Us
- Contact Us
- Gallery
- Home
- Products

For mobile:

- Contact Us
- Home

## To open a Theme Layout

1 On the **File** menu, click **Startup Wizard...**

2 In the Create section, click **Use Design Template**.

3 In the **Create New Site From Template** dialog:

- Browse the **Theme Layouts** category and select the desktop or mobile layout you want to use.

- Choose a **Colour Scheme** from the drop-down list.

  You can choose from three schemes specially designed to complement the template, or you can apply any of the other colour schemes included with WebPlus.

- In the **Pages** pane, using the check boxes, choose the site pages to include in the layout.

- Click **Open**.

The following pages provide previews of WebPlus X6's **Theme Layout** templates populated with example pictures.*

*Articles, Links and Terms & Conditions pages not shown

# Active

Desktop Template

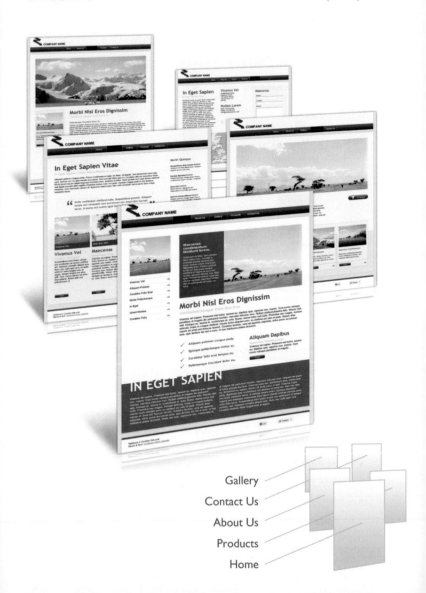

Gallery

Contact Us

About Us

Products

Home

Mobile Template

Contact Us

Home

**Colour Schemes**

Active 01

Active 02

Active 03

# Arctic

Desktop Template

Gallery

Contact Us

About Us

Products

Home

Mobile Template

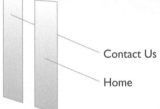

Contact Us

Home

**Colour Schemes**

Arctic 01

Arctic 02

Arctic 03

# **Beta**

Desktop Template

Gallery

Contact Us

About Us

Products

Home

Mobile Template

Contact Us

Home

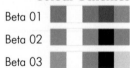

**Colour Schemes**

Beta 01

Beta 02

Beta 03

# Bygone

Desktop Template

Gallery

Contact Us

About Us

Products

Home

Mobile Template

Contact Us

Home

## Colour Schemes

Bygone 01

Bygone 02

Bygone 03

# **Clean**

Desktop Template

Gallery

Contact Us

About Us

Products

Home

Mobile Template

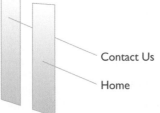

Contact Us

Home

## Colour Schemes

Clean 01

Clean 02

Clean 03

# Clouds

Desktop Template

Gallery

Contact Us

About Us

Products

Home

Mobile Template

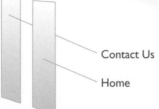

Contact Us

Home

**Colour Schemes**

Clouds 01

Clouds 02

Clouds 03

# **Decor**

Desktop Template

Gallery

Contact Us

About Us

Products

Home

Mobile Template

Contact Us

Home

**Colour Schemes**

Decor 01

Decor 02

Decor 03

# Doodle

Desktop Template

Gallery

Contact Us

About Us

Products

Home

Mobile Template

Contact Us

Home

## Colour Schemes

Doodle 01

Doodle 02

Doodle 03

# Dribble

Desktop Template

Gallery

Contact Us

About Us

Products

Home

Mobile Template

Contact Us

Home

 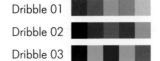

# Eco

Desktop Template

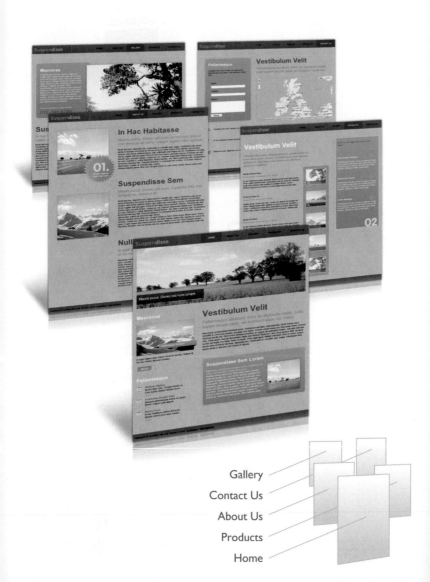

Gallery

Contact Us

About Us

Products

Home

Mobile Template

Contact Us

Home

**Colour Schemes**

Eco 01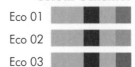

Eco 02

Eco 03

# Editorial

Desktop Template

Gallery

Contact Us

About Us

Products

Home

Mobile Template

Contact Us

Home

**Colour Schemes**

Editorial 01

Editorial 02

Editorial 03

# Factory

Desktop Template

Gallery

Contact Us

About Us

Products

Home

Mobile Template

Contact Us

Home

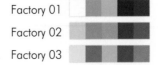

**Colour Schemes**

Factory 01

Factory 02

Factory 03

# Globose

Desktop Template

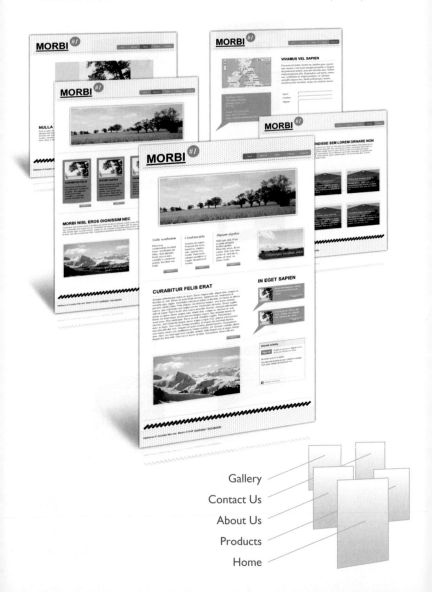

Gallery

Contact Us

About Us

Products

Home

Mobile Template

Contact Us

Home

**Colour Schemes**

Globose 01

Globose 02

Globose 03

# **Ledger**

Desktop Template

Gallery

Contact Us

About Us

Products

Home

Mobile Template

Contact Us

Home

**Colour Schemes**

Ledger 01

Ledger 02

Ledger 03

# Mode

Desktop Template

Gallery

Contact Us

About Us

Products

Home

Mobile Template

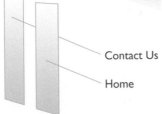

Contact Us

Home

**Colour Schemes**

Mode 01

Mode 02

Mode 03

# Natural

Desktop Template

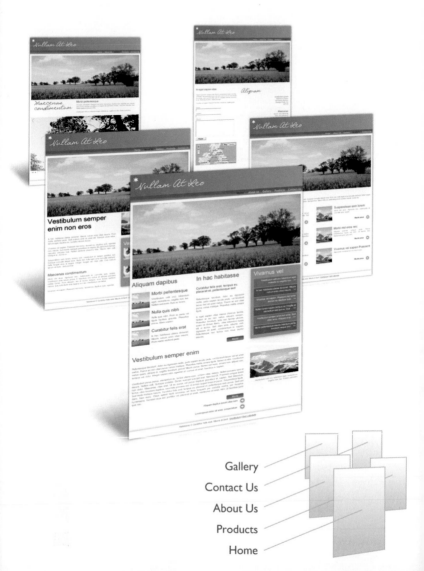

Gallery

Contact Us

About Us

Products

Home

Mobile Template

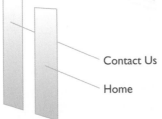

Contact Us

Home

## Colour Schemes

| | |
|---|---|
| Natural 01 | |
| Natural 02 | |
| Natural 03 | |

# Nature

Desktop Template

Gallery

Contact Us

About Us

Products

Home

Mobile Template

Contact Us

Home

## Colour Schemes

Nature 01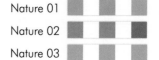

Nature 02

Nature 03

# Pop

Desktop Template

Gallery

Contact Us

About Us

Products

Home

Mobile Template

Contact Us

Home

## Colour Schemes

Pop 01

Pop 02

Pop 03

# Quote

Desktop Template

Gallery

Contact Us

About Us

Products

Home

Mobile Template

Contact Us

Home

**Colour Schemes**

Quote 01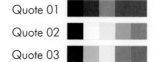

Quote 02

Quote 03

# Renovate

Desktop Template

Gallery

Contact Us

About Us

Products

Home

Mobile Template

Contact Us

Home

## Colour Schemes

Renovate 01

Renovate 02

Renovate 03

# Ribbon

Desktop Template

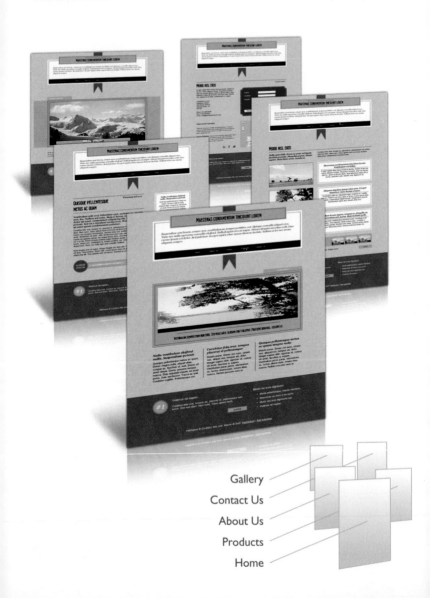

Gallery

Contact Us

About Us

Products

Home

Mobile Template

Contact Us

Home

## Colour Schemes

Ribbon 01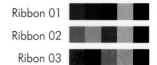

Ribbon 02

Ribon 03

# Rugged

Desktop Template

Gallery

Contact Us

About Us

Products

Home

Mobile Template

Contact Us

Home

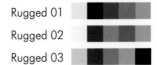

**Colour Schemes**

Rugged 01

Rugged 02

Rugged 03

# Shabby

Desktop Template

Gallery

Contact Us

About Us

Products

Home

Mobile Template

Contact Us

Home

**Colour Schemes**

Shabby 01

Shabby 02

Shabby 03

# Solid

Desktop Template

Gallery

Contact Us

About Us

Products

Home

Mobile Template

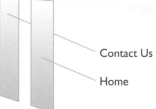

Contact Us

Home

**Colour Schemes**

Solid 01

Solid 02

Solid 03

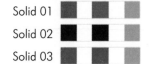

# Spiro

Desktop Template

Gallery

Contact Us

About Us

Products

Home

Mobile Template

Contact Us

Home

## Colour Schemes

Spiro 01

Spiro 02

Spiro 03

# Stitch

Desktop Template

Gallery

Contact Us

About Us

Products

Home

Mobile Template

Contact Us

Home

## Colour Schemes

Stitch 01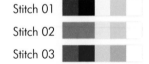

Stitch 02

Stitch 03

# Tabs

Gallery

Contact Us

About Us

Products

Home

Mobile Template

Contact Us

Home

## Colour Schemes

Tabs 01

Tabs 02

Tabs 03

# Tickle

Desktop Template

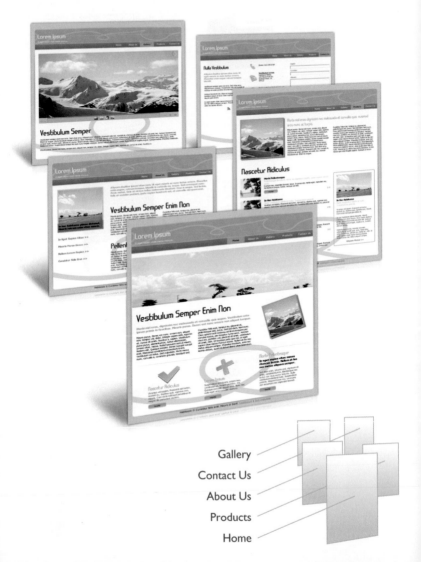

Gallery

Contact Us

About Us

Products

Home

Mobile Template

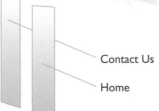

Contact Us

Home

## Colour Schemes

Tickle 01

Tickle 02

Tickle 03

# Trace

Desktop Template

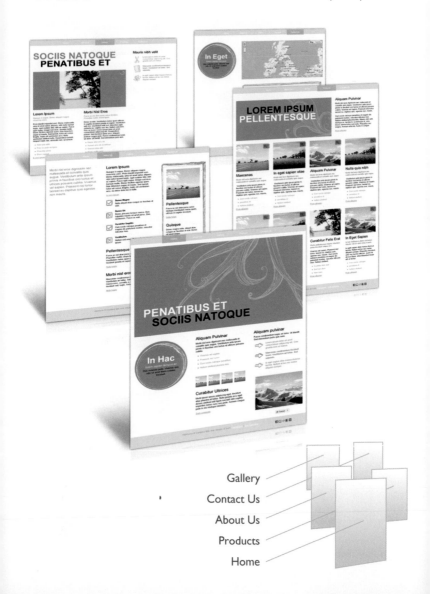

Gallery

Contact Us

About Us

Products

Home

Mobile Template

Contact Us

Home

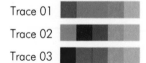

**Colour Schemes**

Trace 01

Trace 02

Trace 03

# Vintage

Desktop Template

Gallery

Contact Us

About Us

Products

Home

Mobile Template

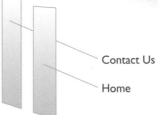

Contact Us

Home

**Colour Schemes**

| | |
|---|---|
| Vintage 01 | |
| Vintage 02 | |
| Vintage 03 | |

# Pro Templates

WebPlus provides a selection of **Pro Templates** that you can use as starting points for your own sites.

Available from the Startup Wizard, the **Pro Templates** are categorized templates containing royalty-free pictures which can be adopted to fast-track you to your completed site. You just need to personalize placeholder text, then publish!

## To open a Pro Template:

1   On the **File** menu, click **Startup Wizard...**

2   In the Create section, click **Use Design Template**.

3   In the **Create** New Site From Template dialog:

- Browse the **WebPlus X6 Pro Templates** category and select the template you want to use.

- Choose a **Colour Scheme** from the drop-down list.

  You can choose from three schemes specially designed to complement the template, or you can apply any of the other colour schemes included with WebPlus.

- In the **Pages** pane, using the check boxes, choose the site pages to include in the layout.

- Click **Open**.

The following pages provide previews of the **Pro Templates** provided with WebPlus X6.

# Designer Blog

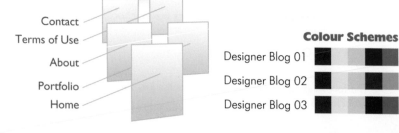

Contact

Terms of Use

About

Portfolio

Home

**Colour Schemes**

Designer Blog 01

Designer Blog 02

Designer Blog 03

# Family Pictures

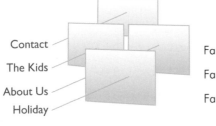

Contact

The Kids

About Us

Holiday

## Colour Schemes

Family Pictures 01

Family Pictures 02

Family Pictures 03

# Finance

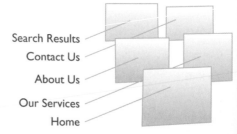

Search Results

Contact Us

About Us

Our Services

Home

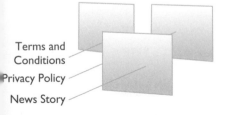

Terms and
Conditions

Privacy Policy

News Story

**Colour Schemes**

Finance 01

Finance 02

Finance 03

# Painter & Decorator

Contact

About

Services

Home

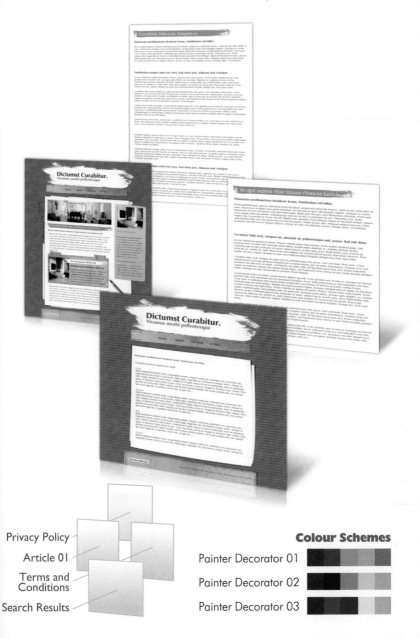

Privacy Policy

Article 01

Terms and
Conditions

Search Results

**Colour Schemes**

Painter Decorator 01

Painter Decorator 02

Painter Decorator 03

# Real Estate - Business

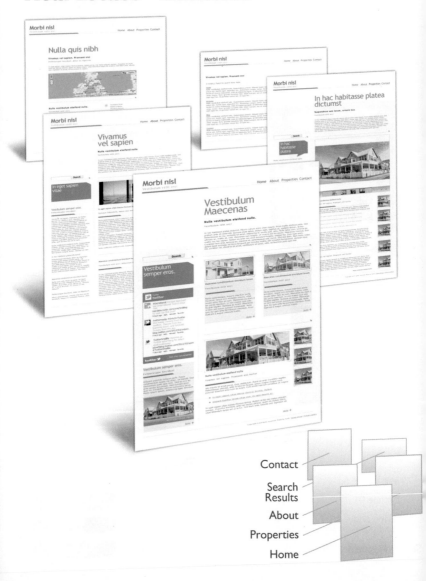

Contact

Search Results

About

Properties

Home

**Colour Schemes**

Real Estate 01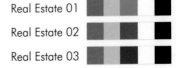

Terms of Use

Privacy Policy

News